To

....

From

....

Date

....

Blessed
Is She
Who Believes

RAE SIMONS

Blessed Is She Who Believes

Devotions and Prayers for Women

BARBOUR
PUBLISHING

Member of the
Evangelical Christian
Publishers Association

Introduction

As Christians, we often talk about belief—and yet, even as we acknowledge our belief in God, our minds are constantly exposed to the beliefs of the world around us. We can easily absorb these societal beliefs, often failing to realize they may not be compatible with our belief in God and His promises.

Our beliefs are important. They shape our attitudes, our behaviors, our professional lives, and our relationships. Researchers have shown, for example, that if we believe we're capable and competent, we're more likely to notice and seek out opportunities that help us attain our dream jobs. Psychologists have found that our beliefs also influence others' behaviors. When we believe others are worthy of love, they are more likely to behave in lovable ways; when we believe someone has the potential to accomplish something, she is likely to perform better. Researchers have also discovered that our beliefs about aging influence what we experience as we grow older; people who expect old age to be miserable complain of more pain and challenges than do people who believe their older years can be filled with new possibilities.

In the pages of this book, you'll have the opportunity to become more aware of your own beliefs, noticing where they line up with scripture and where they may be contrary to God's path. And as your belief in God's promises becomes clearer, you'll find yourself richly blessed in ways you may never have anticipated!

Pregnant with Belief

All around us we observe a pregnant creation. The difficult times of pain throughout the world are simply birth pangs. But it's not only around us; it's within us. The Spirit of God is arousing us within. We're also feeling the birth pangs. . . . That is why waiting does not diminish us, any more than waiting diminishes a pregnant mother. We are enlarged in the waiting. . . . The longer we wait, the larger we become, and the more joyful our expectancy. Meanwhile, the moment we get tired in the waiting, God's Spirit is right alongside helping us along. . . . He knows us far better than we know ourselves, knows our pregnant condition, and keeps us present before God.
ROMANS 8:22–27 MSG

The Holy Spirit is the wind that blows through our world, breathing blessing into everything that exists. As you open yourself to Him, He will breathe into you as well. You need not worry about your weakness or mistakes, for the Spirit will make up for them. His creative power will pray through you, work through you, and bring new life into being through you. As your belief allows the Spirit to bless you, your entire life will become a place where new blessings grow and emerge into the world.

Spirit, I pray that my belief in Your presence will grow ever stronger.

Belief in God's Unconditional Love

GOD. . .relishes integrity.
PROVERBS 11:20 MSG

The Hebrew word that is translated as "integrity" in this verse means "wholeness, completeness, fullness, entirety." This is the sort of integrity that delights God. He wants you to be whole, inside and out, and He wants your inner fullness to be expressed in your external life. This means you no longer need to worry about others' opinions of you, hiding parts of yourself away for fear that others won't understand you. God is delighted by the full expression of your inner being. Believe that God will bless you just for being you, and He will use you—the *real* you—to bless others as well!

Help me, God, to become confident that You love me just the way I am.

The Gift of Friendship

*Wounds from a sincere friend are better
than many kisses from an enemy.*
PROVERBS 27:6 NLT

Talking with a friend, sharing your life with someone who understands, is one of life's great blessings. After you talk with a wise friend, life usually makes more sense. Seemingly unsolvable problems no longer seem as overwhelming. A faithful friend's words—even when you don't want to hear them!—can help you understand yourself and can also point you toward the eternal meaning that's hidden in your life. Friendship teaches you new perspectives. It strengthens your belief in God's power and allows you to see yourself as God sees you.

*Thank You, heavenly Friend, for the earthly friendships You
have given me. Please use my friends to nurture my belief
in You—and use me to encourage my friends as well.*

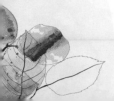

11

Resting in Belief

*And we know that in all things God works for the good of those
who love him, who have been called according to his purpose.*
ROMANS 8:28 NIV

When catastrophe strikes your life, you're faced with the reality of how fragile life truly is. There you were, going along like normal, when without warning something painful happened. Your sense of safety and security was shattered. Life suddenly feels shaky, as though danger is lurking around every corner. Your belief in God's love and power is shaken.

But regardless of your feelings in this moment, God's love remains strong and creative. The same amazing energy that made the world is still at work in every event of your life. What seems like catastrophe will be swept up by His power and made into something that—somehow, in some way—will bless you and those you love. You can rest in that belief!

*Lord, when life seems frightening and unpredictable, remind me
that Your creative power is always at work, weaving together even
life's challenges and disasters into a fabric of blessing. As my belief
in You is tested by life's painful events, may it grow sturdier.*

Initiative and Belief

She looks over a field and buys it, then,
with money she's put aside, plants a garden.
Proverbs 31:16 msg

God doesn't expect you to just sit around waiting for His blessings to drop into your life. Sometimes, He wants you to be proactive—to initiate wise changes in the world around you—instead of merely reacting to problems as they come along. You might, for example, set a goal to eat healthier—so you research options, make a plan, believe in the outcome, and take action. You don't just wait for God to magically change your diet. You take the initiative, and then you believe God will bless your efforts. And He will.

God of power, I ask for Your wisdom as I examine my life. Show me the changes that need to be made. Direct me toward productive and effective decisions. May each of my actions reflect my belief in Your love.

Encouraged to Believe

If your gift is to encourage others, be encouraging.
ROMANS 12:8 NLT

The word *encourage* comes from Latin words that mean to put heart or inner strength into someone. The Greek word originally used in this verse adds even deeper meaning, for it implies that the person who encourages others comes close by their side; she becomes so intimate with another person that her words are trustworthy, motivating, and inspiring. Others can believe in what she says. When God encourages you, His own heart reaches out to you, and His strength becomes yours. He enters into an intimate relationship with you so that you can have confidence in His promises. Then, as you rely on this blessing, you will be empowered to reach out to those around you, lending them your own heart and strength as you inspire them to believe in the power of God's love.

Thank You, God, for all the ways You encourage me and bless me. May I in turn encourage and bless others.

Belief in Eternity

"There is plenty of room for you in my Father's home. If that weren't so, would I have told you that I'm on my way to get a room ready for you?"
JOHN 14:2 MSG

People have various beliefs about eternity, but the fact is none of us *knows* exactly what lies on the other side of death's dark door. But you can be certain of this: death will take you home. Jesus promised that. He wouldn't have said it just to make us feel better, because Jesus wasn't one for telling polite lies. He didn't make up stories just to make Himself look better either. So you can rest in the belief that right now He is getting your home in heaven ready for you, filling it with everything you need to be happy. When the day comes that you enter the door, you'll find it's exactly right for you—the place you've always longed for.

Jesus, I'm grateful for Your promises. When death seems like something dark and frightening, help me believe that it is a homegoing. Thank You that You are creating the perfect home for me for all eternity.

Belief in the Darkness

Why am I discouraged? Why is my heart so sad? I will put my hope in God!
PSALM 42:5 NLT

Thousands of years ago, the psalmist who wrote these words expressed the same feelings you have today. Some days you just feel down in the dumps. The world looks dark, everything seems to be going wrong, and your heart is sad. Those feelings are part of the human condition; they're perfectly normal, but they can shake your belief in God's plan for your life. Like the psalmist so long ago, take a moment to remind yourself that God is unchanged by cloudy skies and gloomy hearts. His blessings are always the same, as bright and hopeful as ever, no matter how life may seem.

When my heart is sad and life seems overwhelming,
bless me, I pray, with confidence in You.

Belief in Possibility

Is any thing too hard for the LORD?
GENESIS 18:14 KJV

One night God told Abraham to look up at the night sky and count the stars. There were too many stars for Abraham to count, of course—and then God made an amazing promise to Abraham: "You'll have as many children as there are stars in the sky" (see Genesis 15:5). At the time, though, Abraham and his wife, Sarah, had no children at all; and they were old, much too old to have children. Abraham might have thought he had dreamed his conversation with God. He would have found it hard to believe in a promise so enormous. And yet God kept His word. When Abraham was one hundred and Sarah was ninety, their son, Isaac, was born. Isaac was the beginning of the Jewish people, who now are more than can be counted.

When you look at the challenging situations in your own life, remember what God did for Abraham and Sarah. Believe in what God can do. The word *impossible* is not in His vocabulary!

*God of Abraham and Sarah, help me believe in
Your power of possibility at work in my life.*

Believe in Self-Control!

Stop being angry! Turn from your rage!
Do not lose your temper—it only leads to harm.
PSALM 37:8 NLT

Some people believe that feeling anger is a sin. Others believe they are powerless to control their own angry feelings. Anger is a normal and healthy emotion, and even Jesus got angry during His time on earth. But this verse gives you good advice for managing anger: when you get mad, believe you have the power to turn away from your anger, rather than dwell on it or wallow in it. Instead of feeding it until it explodes, you can practice letting it go. First, of course, you may need to acknowledge your angry feelings. Don't try to stuff them away and pretend they're not there. But then give them to God. This mental habit will keep anger from being the driver in your life. It will create a space for healthy attitudes about anger to grow—and it will protect you and those around you from words and actions that could be hurtful. Believe that God can be the container that holds your temper!

Thank You, Lord, that You understand all my emotions, including my anger. I ask You to help me practice self-control. Remind me I have the power to give my anger to You, rather than letting it run my life.

Loving Friends

Dear friends, let us love one another, for love comes from God.
1 JOHN 4:7 NIV

Left to yourself, you might spend much of your time spinning around in your own head, buzzing in tiny circles like flies caught inside a window. Friendship throws open a window and lets those dizzy flies escape. It lets in the fresh air of new beliefs, perspectives, and ideas. Through your friends, you catch a glimpse of God's love. He speaks to you through their voices. He loves you with their smiles and kindness and understanding. Each time they send you a text or email, each time you sit and talk with them over a cup of tea or coffee, and each time you get the giggles over something one of your friends said to you, you are experiencing God's love. And as you return that love to your friends, you allow God to use you to bless them too. Your belief in God will begin to widen and extend itself into the world.

Thank You, heavenly Friend, for the human friends You have brought into my life. I am so grateful for the love You show me through the friendship we share. Through them, I am learning to believe in You more deeply.

Belief Instead of Worry

Instead of worrying, pray. Let petitions and praises shape your worries into prayers, letting God know your concerns. Before you know it, a sense of God's wholeness, everything coming together for good, will come and settle you down. It's wonderful what happens when Christ displaces worry at the center of your life.

PHILIPPIANS 4:6–7 MSG

If you're like many women, worry just seems to come naturally to you. Especially on sleepless nights, you may lie awake wondering: *Are my loved ones safe? Will my family have enough money for what we need? Will I do a good job at work this week? Will my friends accept me if I speak what's on my mind? Will I be able to keep up with all my responsibilities? How will I know the right decisions to make?* Anxieties have a habit of piling up, one on top of another, robbing you of your confidence in God.

But anxiety can be transformed into prayer. Each time you find yourself fretting over something, turn that specific set of circumstances over to God. As you make this practice a habit, the presence of Christ will take the place of anxiety in your mind. Your belief in God will grow deeper roots.

Thank You, Jesus, that I can give all my worries to You.
I believe You are strong enough to handle them all.

Belief in Justice

Speak up for those who cannot speak for themselves;
ensure justice for those being crushed.
PROVERBS 31:8 NLT

There's a belief going around that says all we need to do is think positive thoughts, and blessings will just miraculously appear. In reality, however, God uses His creation—and each of us—as the channels through which His blessings flow into the world. When we keep silent about injustice, believing that it's not our job to get involved, we can block the flow of divine blessing, causing hatred and oppression to prevail. Sometimes, we even use our religious beliefs to justify our lack of action. We judge people with different beliefs and appearances harshly, and we close our ears to other perspectives and new information.

But God wants you to pay attention, to notice who is being crushed and to be willing to express the perspectives of those our society has too often silenced. Your beliefs about politics, religion, or anything else should never be more important to you than your belief in love. Love is the way God changes the world.

Use me, Lord, I pray, to carry Your justice and love into the world.
Show me what I can do to help the silenced and the crushed.
Correct any false beliefs I have about others, and may I never
permit my ideas or opinions to block the flow of Your love.

God's Economy

*When we get together, I want to encourage you in your
faith, but I also want to be encouraged by yours.*
ROMANS 1:12 NLT

In the world's economy, we pay a price in order to receive something
we want; we have to give up something in order to get something.
That belief is deeply ingrained in our minds, but that's not the way
things work in God's economy, where giving and receiving are linked
together. We need to be open to this divine belief, allowing it to
replace what the world tells us. As we accept that whatever good
we do for another person is good for us as well, we will begin to
understand that we are truly connected to each other, like parts of
a body. What blesses me will ultimately bless you—and vice versa.
When we encourage others, we too will be encouraged.

*Teach me, God of love, not to be stingy with my resources (whether they
are physical or emotional). May I share the blessings You give me with
others, believing that as I encourage others, I too will be encouraged.*

The Willingness to Learn

*Intelligent people are always ready to learn.
Their ears are open for knowledge.*
PROVERBS 18:15 NLT

In one way or another, most of us rely on our intelligence to get us through life. If we're truly intelligent, though, we'll remember that no matter how many years it's been since we were in school, we're never done learning. We need to be open to new ideas, willing to give up old, stale ways of thinking; we need to be willing to accept the possibility that we could be wrong. And then, as we open our ears to new information, we'll find we learn more and more about God and His plan for us. His blessings will be revealed to us in ways we never expected. Our belief in Him will spread out into new dimensions.

Show me, Lord, where I've closed my mind to new ideas. Help me be willing to be surprised by something new. Give me the courage to let go of old ways of looking at things so You can reveal to me more about Your kingdom. Remind me that my belief is in You and Your love, rather than my own opinions.

Stop Worrying!

"Can any one of you by worrying add a single hour to your life?"
MATTHEW 6:27 NIV

On the nights when you have insomnia, you probably don't lie awake filled with hope and happiness. If you're like most of us, you're much more likely to lie there consumed with worries. Instead of imagining all the wonderful things God has in store for you, you may find yourself picturing scenarios of doom and gloom. *What if such-and-such happens,* you think, and then you build a complete picture of just how terrible that "such-and-such" might turn out to be. Your worries shake your belief in God's love and providence. But the Bible says that prayer can be your antidote to worry. When you turn your worrying into prayer, your belief in God's love will grow stronger. As you fix your thoughts on God and His promises, your outlook will change. You'll anticipate blessing instead of disaster. You'll be confident that God has everything under control.

*God, when worries threaten to overwhelm me, remind me to turn
my thoughts away from images of disaster and instead anticipate
all the blessings You have in store for me. May worry no longer
have the power to shake my belief in Your providence.*

Belief and Laughter

A cheerful heart is a good medicine.
PROVERBS 17:22 NRSV

Belief in God and a good sense of humor may seem to have very little to do with one another. As Christians, we may be convinced we need to maintain a sober and serious outlook to be consistent with our religious beliefs. Besides, keeping a sense of humor and a positive perspective isn't easy, not when life is so filled with stress and responsibilities and challenges. The long-ago author of Proverbs 17:22, however, knew the same truth that modern-day psychologists know: Laughter relaxes tension. It allows your body and soul to take a deep, healing breath. It lifts you up when circumstances are pulling you down. It gives you a clearer vision, so that you can once more believe in God's grace and love.

God of joy, thank You for the gift of laughter. When life seems overwhelming, give me reasons to smile. Remind me that a healthy belief in You will never get in the way of my sense of humor. Help me to even be willing to laugh at myself.

Belief in God's Victory

*When you go to war against your enemies and see horses and chariots
and an army greater than yours, do not be afraid of them, because
the LORD your God, who brought you up out of Egypt, will be with you.
When you are about to go into battle, the priest shall come forward and
address the army. He shall say: "Hear, Israel: Today you are going into
battle against your enemies. Do not be fainthearted or afraid; do not
panic or be terrified by them. For the LORD your God is the one who goes
with you to fight for you against your enemies to give you victory."*
DEUTERONOMY 20:1–4 NIV

Okay, so you're not likely to ever face an army of horses and chariots—but these verses can still speak to your life. After all, some days the challenges in your life can seem as terrifying and dangerous as any battlefield. So the next time that happens, follow the advice given here in Deuteronomy. First, like the Israelites who recalled how God had helped them escape from Egypt, you too can remember all that God has done for you in the past. Next, remind yourself that God is the One who will fight your battles through you and around you. You can believe in His victory over whatever challenges you face today.

*God of power, thank You that You are ready and willing to fight the battles
in my life. May my belief in Your strength make room for Your victories.*

Listening

Fools think their own way is right, but the wise listen to others.
Proverbs 12:15 nlt

The Bible is full of practical advice, and the book of Proverbs in particular teaches us ways to get along better with others. The ability to listen is one of the building blocks of any good relationship, whether it's with our spouses, with friends, with our children, or with God. All too often, though, we may find ourselves focusing on the constant chatter inside our own heads, rather than listening for what God wants us to hear. Or we may become so focused on our own beliefs that we forget to look outside ourselves to the living world around us. When we cut through our preoccupation with our own thoughts, however, we can begin to listen on a deeper level—and we will gain deeper insights about life, others, ourselves, and God. Our belief in God will be expressed in practical outcomes in the world around us.

*Thank You, Lord, that You always listen to me. Teach me
to be a better listener to You and to those around me.
I believe You have much You want me to learn.*

The Persistence of Belief

"Ask and it will be given to you; seek and you will find;
knock and the door will be opened to you."
MATTHEW 7:7 NIV

This is a wonderful promise that Jesus gave us. But what if instead of the door opening, it gets slammed in your face? What if you ask and ask and ask, and nothing ever seems to change? How can you continue to believe in God's promises when everything around you seems to be going wrong? Scripture promises that God continues to bless you, even when it seems you're surrounded by disappointment. When God doesn't answer the way you thought He would, follow the advice found in the book of Proverbs: "Trust in the LORD with all your heart and lean not on your own understanding" (3:5 NIV). God's perspective is more accurate than yours, and His blessings are on their way. So, while you wait, be patient and don't give up. Be persistent in your belief!

God, I'm going to keep asking, seeking, and knocking, no matter
how long You seem to be taking to answer me. I believe You
are blessing me even now, during this time of waiting.

Trust

"I will trust and not be afraid."
ISAIAH 12:2 NIV

Another word for "belief in God" might be *trust*—the total confidence that God loves you and will never harm you. Trust is what allows you to be vulnerable with God and others; it makes intimacy possible; and it is essential to your spiritual and emotional well-being. You first learned to trust as a baby, and that most basic level of trust is the foundation for all your relationships, including your relationship with God. But sometimes parents fail to teach their children how to trust. If your parents hurt you, you may find it hard to trust others, including God. Or maybe a close friend or a spouse damaged your trust later in life. Now you might find yourself constantly on guard, trying to protect yourself against hurt. This lack of trust can come between you and the blessings God longs to give you.

If you relate to any of these words, don't condemn yourself to a life of distrust. God wants to heal you from the wounds you have received in the past. He wants to make you whole so you can believe His promises. He wants to teach you that He is trustworthy so His love can be the foundation for healthy relationships with others too.

*Lord, find the wounded places inside me and heal them with
Your love. Restore to me the blessings of trust in You.*

Humility and Pride

"God blesses those who are humble, for they will inherit the whole earth."
MATTHEW 5:5 NLT

Do you ever compare yourself to others around you—and when you do, you find you never seem to measure up? Maybe you wish you could be smarter or funnier, prettier or thinner. You wish that you could accomplish as much as your colleague does in a day, or that you could make as much money as your friend does, or that you were as thin as your sister. You wish you were calmer or more creative. All this wishing shapes your beliefs about yourself. And you might *think* you've ended up with a belief about yourself that is the exact opposite of pride; you might equate your self-criticism with humility. But self-doubting your own worth is not what God wants for you. When He hears your mind filled with self-dissatisfaction, He longs for you to simply take from Him the gift of yourself. He wants you to humbly accept yourself—both the good parts and the less good—and then offer them all back to Him. When you make peace with being the person you are, He promises to bless that person! You can replace your belief that you're not good enough with the confidence that you are infinitely precious to God.

Loving God, help me be humble enough to accept my imperfections.
Remind me that I don't need to be better than others for You to love me.

Faith

Jesus immediately reached out and grabbed him.
"You have so little faith," Jesus said. "Why did you doubt me?"
MATTHEW 14:31 NLT

You can read the whole story in Matthew 14. Jesus was walking on the water, and Peter, impetuous as always, jumped out of the boat and joined Him. Peter was doing just fine, walking along on the surface of the sea, his eyes fixed on Jesus. But then he looked down. He saw his feet stepping over the waves—and instantly, he started to sink. In that moment, he forgot everything he believed about Jesus. He was positive he was going to drown.

Jesus didn't let him, of course. He reached out and saved Peter. And He'll do the same for you, each and every time you find yourself swamped with doubts, beginning to sink into life's depths. "Why do you doubt Me?" He'll ask you. "I will *never* let you sink. Have faith in Me!"

When doubts torment me, Lord Jesus, strengthen
my heart. Bless me with belief in You.

Believing in God's Commandments

Whoever keeps commandments keeps their life.
PROVERBS 19:16 NIV

Do you connect the word *commandments* with negative, authoritarian impositions on your life? In reality, God's commandments are always intended to bless your life with greater depth, breadth, and all-around well-being. They lead you away from self-destructive behaviors and attitudes; they keep you from sabotaging your relationships or your finances. Like all human beings, you will, of course, make mistakes sometimes; but scripture also shows you the way to remedy what you can. God's ways lead to growth and health, physically, emotionally, and spiritually. As you believe in them and follow them, you are actually protecting yourself from harm. You are putting yourself in places where God's blessings can freely flow into your life.

Father, teach me to believe in Your way, for I know it leads to ever-greater blessings in my life. Thank You for always wanting what is best for me.

The Blessing of Belief

For we live by believing and not by seeing.
2 CORINTHIANS 5:7 NLT

Modern-day Western culture was shaped by the scientific method, which tells us that only what can be seen, measured, and proved is truly real. But twenty-first-century scientists know reality is far bigger than what our five senses can take in. Our own hearts know this as well. Every day, we depend on the things we can't see and yet believe—our faith in God and in our friends and family, our commitment to give ourselves to God and others—and it is these invisible beliefs that daily bless our lives with richness and depth.

Lord of love, I can't see You—but I believe You are present with me: in the world around me and within my own heart. I cannot prove Your presence, and yet my belief in You shapes my entire life. Expand my belief in You, I pray. May it grow stronger and more certain. Bless me with a growing belief in You.

Belief and Prayer

"That person can pray to God and find favor with him,
they will see God's face and shout for joy."
J**OB** 33:26 NIV

Is it ever hard for you to believe in the power of prayer? Do you wonder if you are just talking to the air? Probably every human being who ever prayed has had that feeling at times—and yet the Bible tells us again and again that we all need to pray. It's not something that God needs; it's what *you* need. Praying is a way for you to experience your connection with God's Spirit. A regular prayer practice strengthens belief, lifts your heart, and diminishes discouragement. Your faith will grow, and you will become more aware of the many blessings God gives to you. What's more, your spiritual sight will be sharpened, and you will begin to see from God's perspective. None of these things happen instantly, but as you make prayer a lifetime habit, your belief in God's promises will become a firm foundation that gives stability to your entire life.

God, when I doubt the power of prayer, remind me that I need to pray
in order to experience all the blessings You are longing to give me.
Even on my busiest days, may my heart and mind remain connected
with Your Spirit in a constant stream of prayer that continues in the
background of my mind. May prayer unite my heart with Yours.

Believe in God's Kindness!

The LORD is righteous in everything he does; he is filled with kindness.
PSALM 145:17 NLT

The word *kind* comes from the same roots as *kin*. They're both words that originally had to do with family, with intimate shared relationships like the ones that exist between members of the same family. This is what God shows us: the kindness of a good father, the gentleness of a good mother, the understanding of a brother or sister. In Hebrew, the word that's translated as "kind" has to do with mercy and courtesy—the willingness to put oneself last, to forgive and not insist on one's own rights. When you consider the depth of meanings contained within this word, you gain a better picture of the kindness God longs to show you!

Thank You, Lord, that You are always loving, gentle, merciful, and forgiving. You are never selfish or harsh. I believe in Your kindness!

Joy and Amazement

We were filled with laughter, and we sang for joy. And the other nations said, "What amazing things the LORD has done for them."
PSALM 126:2 NLT

Life is truly amazing. Each day is filled with wonderful blessing. God's love touches you in so many ways, from the sun on your face to each person you encounter, from the love of your friends and family to the satisfaction of your work. Pay attention. Believe that each blessing in your life is a love token from God. Notice the little blessings as well as the bigger ones. Make room for joy as a part of your daily life. Let people hear you laugh more. Don't hide your joy, for it is a witness to God's love and blessing, letting people know what you believe about God. You have an amazing source of joy in your life and heart!

Thank You, amazing God, for all the blessings You shower on me. Remind me to see joy faster than I see sorrow in my life. Teach me to believe in Your joyful love. I don't want to take for granted all the amazing things You do for me, each and every day.

Belief in God's Rules

The precepts of the LORD are right, giving joy to the heart.
The commands of the LORD are radiant, giving light to the eyes.
PSALM 19:8 NIV

When you were a child, did you ever feel as though your parents' rules had no purpose but to make you miserable? Did you wonder if they *always* said no whenever you really wanted to do something? You may not have understood that your parents' love was behind their rules. Now, as an adult, do you ever find yourself having the same attitude toward God's rules? Do you wonder if a life of sin might be easier, more fun? In reality, it's just the opposite. God always wants what will give you joy. His rules are designed to make you shine. His only motivation is to bless you with a fuller, richer, more complete and healthy life. Can you believe that?

God, I believe You always know what is best for me. You bless
me with rules that lead to life and love and fulfillment.

Enemies

"You're familiar with the old written law, 'Love your friend,' and its unwritten companion, 'Hate your enemy.' I'm challenging that. I'm telling you to love your enemies. Let them bring out the best in you, not the worst. When someone gives you a hard time, respond with the supple moves of prayer, for then you are working out of your true selves, your God-created selves. . . . Live generously and graciously toward others, the way God lives toward you."
MATTHEW 5:43–45, 48 MSG

Sometimes Christians ignore what Jesus says here in the Gospel of Matthew. We make enemies out of the people we don't approve of, the people who disagree with what we believe, who have different politics, different values, different ideas. We might deny that we treat these people like enemies—but do we really act as though we love them? Do we offer them the best of ourselves? Do we pray for them with all our energy? And if we *do* pray for them, are we only praying that they will change their minds and think like we do? Or are we truly praying that God will bless them, no matter what? Jesus tells us we can't enter into our own God-given identities if we don't start treating everyone, including our enemies, with the same love and generosity God has shown us. He wants us to believe He will use even our "enemies" to bless us.

Lord, remind me that You want to bless me through the people I don't like, the people I disagree with, the people I disapprove of. I believe You will teach me more about You, myself, and others as I open my heart to everyone.

Diligence

The desires of the diligent are fully satisfied.
PROVERBS 13:4 NIV

I have no choice in the matter. Perhaps you've said those words when you were faced with a difficult decision. If so, you might have felt trapped by that belief. The truth is you *do* have choices; you just may not be able to see them at first glance. You can ask questions, research your options, consider the pros and cons, and then make a reasonable choice based on the knowledge you have at the time. By your own diligence—following through, taking action, digging in— that boxed-in feeling may disappear, so that you enjoy new freedom. Believe this: God will bless you as you exercise diligence in your life!

God, when I feel like giving up, remind me that You bless diligence. Give me the strength to keep looking until I find the answers that are right for me.

Unknown Blessings

It's only natural to fear the unknown, to feel anxiety as you face the future. Four-year-olds often fear kindergarten. Children sometimes fear adulthood. And adults fear major life changes like a move across the country, a new job, or other new responsibilities. You may fear old age. Almost everyone is afraid of death, the ultimate transition into the unknown. When you look back at your life, though, do you notice that when the change you dreaded actually arrived, you were ready for it? It probably brought you greater freedom, greater satisfaction, greater happiness than ever before. The four-year-old is not ready for kindergarten—but the five-year-old usually is. The ten-year-old is not ready for the responsibilities of adulthood—but the twenty-two-year-old revels in them. And the new job or new home that filled you with anxiety brings with it new friends and new accomplishments that fulfill you in ways you never imagined. Old age has special rewards of its own—and death, that great unknown, will lead you into the presence of God. You don't have to fear the unknown; instead, believe it holds more blessings than you have ever dreamed of!

Lord, I'm so glad You know what the future holds, even though I don't. I believe that just as You have blessed me in the past, You will also bless me in the future. You are not limited by what I can imagine now. The unknown that lies ahead is rich with blessing.

Belief Despite Disappointment

Though the fig tree does not bud and there are no grapes on the vines, though the olive crop fails and the fields produce no food, though there are no sheep in the pen and no cattle in the stalls, yet I will rejoice in the Lord.
HABAKKUK 3:17–18 NIV

Has life disappointed you? Maybe you had hoped to reach a particular milestone by this point in your life, and it hasn't materialized as you imagined; instead, your goal is as far away as ever. You may even have had to face that you will *never* attain this particular goal. Or maybe someone you counted on let you down, and you're disappointed that this individual is not the person you had thought. Or maybe it's your own self that has disappointed you; your failures and weaknesses have forced you to realize you're not the person you always dreamed of being. Disappointment is hard to bear; but when you finally let go of something you were hoping for, God has room to bring something even better into your life. And one thing is certain: no matter what else disappoints you, God never will! When everything else lets you down—when the fig tree doesn't bud, the vines have no grapes, your crops fail, and everything in your life seems empty—you can rest in the sure belief that God still has blessings in store for you.

When disappointment overwhelms me, dear Lord, remind me that You always have something even better planned for me. I believe in Your promises.

Freedom from People-Pleasing

Fearing people is a dangerous trap, but trusting the LORD means safety.
PROVERBS 29:25 NLT

Your friend wants you to do one thing. Your husband suggests something else. Both their ideas are different from what your parents think you should do. You feel torn and confused by their differing opinions. You're afraid that if you do what one person would like, the other will be unhappy with you. You get that familiar pain in the pit of your stomach, the one that makes you doubt yourself and your ability to make a choice on your own. But God doesn't want people-pleasing to rule your life, and you don't have to be afraid of others' opinions. God can help you escape this trap. As you grow closer to Him, His opinion will matter more to you than the opinions of others. As you believe in His absolute love, you will finally be free to be yourself.

God, thank You that You just want me to be myself. You don't want me to spend my life trying to please others. I believe You will bless me as I learn to be true to myself.

God's Unfailing Love

I trust in your unfailing love. I will rejoice because you have rescued me.
PSALM 13:5 NLT

Have you ever done that trust exercise where you're asked to fall backward into another person's arms? It's hard to believe the other person will actually catch you. The decision to let yourself drop is something you have to make up your mind to do, no matter what your emotions tell you, despite your fear. In the same way, you can commit yourself to God's unfailing love. As you make up your mind to trust Him, letting your life drop into His hands, you'll experience new blessings each time His arms keep you from falling. Your belief in God will no longer be something that lives only in your head; it will become the certainty that flows through each aspect of your life.

I am so glad, Lord, that You will never let me crash and break.
Give me the courage to be open to new blessings. Help me
have the strength to believe Your promises more and more.

The Fullness of Life

"I have come that they may have life, and have it to the full."
JOHN 10:10 NIV

Deep down, what do you really believe about life? The life that Jesus described to His followers is wide, deep, rich, and fulfilling. This is the life He wants you to believe in too—a life that is never restricted or narrow. God's love doesn't flow to you in a stingy trickle. Instead, God has blessings in store for you that will fill your life to the brim. Believe in His promises—and you will realize that blessings come to you each moment, day after day, year after year, an abundant, bountiful flood that fills every crack and crevice of your life and then overflows, spreading out from your life into the world around you.

Jesus, thank You for Your promise of a full and abundant life.
I believe in You, and I know You will keep Your promise.

God's Long Arm

Surely the arm of the LORD is not too short to save.
ISAIAH 59:1 NIV

Have you ever noticed that when you have a big problem, God can seem further away than He usually does? That's because your need is taking up all your attention, looming large on the horizon, blocking your vision of God. All you can see is your huge problem filling your entire range of vision. When that happens, it's time to step back and get a new perspective. Scripture says that God's "arm" is long enough to reach past any problem. It is strong enough to reach down into your life to deal with the situation that seems so overwhelming to you. His mighty, outstretched arm will reach down to you and meet you at your point of deepest need. Believe this: absolutely nothing is too hard for God—and He is never too far away to bless you!

Lord, when my problems loom so large that I can't see You, reach past my troubled thoughts and show me Your presence. I believe Your arm is long enough to reach me, no matter the circumstances of my life!

Pride

She senses the worth of her work.
PROVERBS 31:18 MSG

The word *pride* has a range of meanings. For example, there's that old saying "Pride goeth before a fall" (based on Proverbs 16:18). The Bible also says, "The LORD detests all the proud of heart. Be sure of this: They will not go unpunished" (Proverbs 16:5 NIV). The Hebrew word translated as "pride" has to do with setting yourself up higher than others, with claiming that you are more important than those around you. While this kind of pride leads to sin, all too often Christian women have ended up with the wrong beliefs about pride and humility. They believed that humility meant denying their own very real abilities. But Bible verses that speak against pride are not talking about taking honest satisfaction in your work, as Proverbs 31:18 makes clear. Believe in the abilities God has given you and celebrate them. Put them to use. God is delighted to partner with you when you use your abilities to grow and to make the world a better place—and He will bless you with the same delight.

*Thank You, Creator, for all the abilities You have
given me. I take pride in using them for You.*

Christ's Peacemaking

For he himself is our peace, who has made the two groups one and has destroyed the barrier, the dividing wall of hostility.

EPHESIANS 2:14 NIV

When someone does something that irritates you or offends you, do your feelings of justified indignation build inside you, robbing you of your peace? Even if you don't say anything, the hostility is still there. Nothing has been settled, and the argument turns into a barrier between you, breaking your relationship and destroying your peace of mind. That barrier will even come between you and God. It will create beliefs about yourself, about God, and about the world around you that are contrary to God's love. But if you let down the barrier, the Spirit of Christ can enter you. As you stop listening to the voice that insists on your own way, the Spirit will create something new inside you—a state of inner peace and wholeness. Now you'll discover new, constructive roads to peace in the relationship that was giving you trouble. You'll find you no longer look at the other person as separate and opposed to your own needs. Jesus will become your peace, and your belief in His love will be expressed in your life.

Make peace in my life, Jesus. Enter my heart and push out all the selfishness. Fill me with Your willingness to give everything for the sake of love. I believe Your Spirit is at work in my life.

Victorious Love

Overwhelming victory is ours through Christ, who loved us.
ROMANS 8:37 NLT

Do you ever have days when victory seems elusive? When everything you do seems doomed to failure? Meanwhile, the world tells you that success is important, essential even. Countless books have been written on the topic, each one offering yet another secret formula for guaranteeing that success will be yours. Believing that success is essential creates a false reality, however. The truth is everyone experiences failures. Even the heroes of our faith experienced their share of failure. Abraham and Sarah, Elijah and David, Peter and Paul—all knew what it was like to make mistakes. God used even those failures, though, to bring them to the places where He wanted them to be. "Failure should be our teacher, not our undertaker," motivational author Denis Waitley once said. "Failure is delay, not defeat. It is a temporary detour, not a dead end. Failure is something we can avoid only by saying nothing, doing nothing, and being nothing." Don't let the fear of failure paralyze you. Instead, believe that even in the midst of failure, you can still find victory in Christ.

Christ Jesus, thank You that even when I feel like I'm a failure,
You promise me I'm victorious through Your love. May this
belief replace the world's emphasis on external success.

Prosperity

Whoever pursues righteousness and love finds life, prosperity and honor.
PROVERBS 21:21 NIV

We tend to believe that prosperity means material riches. According to MerriamWebster.com, the definition of *prosperity* is "the state of being successful, usually by making a lot of money." Some Christians have even decided that God guarantees them this sort of prosperity. But when the Bible speaks of prosperity, it's referring to a different kind of blessing. The Hebrew word in this verse also refers to God's justice, salvation, and redemption. It has to do with being safe, healthy, and complete, with a sense of physical, emotional, and spiritual well-being. So, as Proverbs 21:21 promises, as you believe in God's righteousness and love, you will be blessed with well-being, inside and out. You will thrive in ways that extend far beyond mere material riches.

Bless me with fullness of life, I pray, Lord. May I experience the well-being You want me to have. Show me if any of my beliefs, behaviors, or attitudes are blocking the flow of Your blessing.

A Double Blessing

At the same time, don't be callous in your exercise of freedom, thoughtlessly stepping on the toes of those who aren't as free as you are. I try my best to be considerate of everyone's feelings in all these matters; I hope you will be, too.
1 CORINTHIANS 10:32–33 MSG

God has blessed you with freedom, and He wants you to claim this gift and make it your own. You no longer need to live trapped by self-doubt or false guilt. God wants you to believe Him when He says you are free. At the same time, though, He wants you to be sensitive to others' feelings and beliefs. Not everyone is at the same place in their spiritual journeys, and some of the people around you may not have yet claimed the full freedom God wants for them. As you follow the Spirit's leading, you'll learn not to trip over other people's beliefs. You won't shove your way through conversations, insisting that your beliefs are the only correct ones. Instead, you will learn to be more aware of other people's reactions. This doesn't mean you surrender your own spiritual freedom to others' narrow minds, legalistic opinions, and limited perspectives—but it does mean you'll let God-given empathy direct your words and actions. As you do so, you'll receive a double blessing: the rewards of both inner freedom and a life of active compassion.

God, I believe You have set me free. May I use the freedom You have given me to bless others also.

Belief in God's Love and Life

Each day the LORD pours his unfailing love upon me, and through each night I sing his songs, praying to God who gives me life.
PSALM 42:8 NLT

Life itself is a blessing. The very blood that flows through your veins, the beat of your heart, the steady hum of your metabolism—all are blessings from God. God's constant and unconditional love pours into the cells of your body; it nourishes you through the food you eat; it surrounds you with the healing benefits of rest as you sleep each night. Like an unborn child who is constantly surrounded by her mother's care, you too live and move within the very being of God. As you become more and more convinced that you are so deeply loved, so intimately cared for, so immersed in blessing, you'll find yourself singing, even in the darkness.

I believe Your love surrounds me, God. I believe it flows through my own body. I believe I can find Your love all around me. I believe in You!

Belief in the Creator of the Universe

Is any thing too hard for the Lord?
GENESIS 18:14 KJV

At one time or another, you've probably run into problems you believed were insurmountable. Your belief put limits on your life. It led to feelings of hopelessness and discouragement. The next time that happens, try spending some time outdoors on a starry night, lying on your back, looking up at the endless reaches of space. It's a good way to get your beliefs back in order. As you gaze at the immensity of the universe, listen for the Spirit's voice: "I created all this. I hold it all in My hands. Nothing is too hard for Me." Your strength has limits, and if you were left on your own, some problems probably would be insurmountable. But God's power has no limits. He has the power and the creativity to lead you forward—through, over, or around every difficult situation. So next time your belief in yourself fails, that's not necessarily a bad thing. Now you can believe in God's strength instead!

Lord of the universe, I believe You created all the mysterious depths of space. You are intimately acquainted with each star and planet, each galaxy and black hole. Nothing is too hard for You, including my own problems!

Helplessness and Belief

"But the tax collector stood at a distance. He would not even look up to heaven, but beat his breast and said, 'God, have mercy on me, a sinner.'"
LUKE 18:13 NIV

You've probably heard the expression "God helps those who help themselves." And while there's a certain truth to the saying (God doesn't want you to sit there expecting a miracle when He's already put the means to accomplish something into your hands), the opposite is also true: *God helps those who are helpless.* He helps those who believe God is their only hope. The tax collector described in this Gospel passage is a good example: He didn't try to prove his own worth. Instead, he threw himself on God's mercy. He didn't let false beliefs about himself come between him and God.

Alcoholics Anonymous teaches that only when a person has hit bottom and finally believes in her own helplessness is she ready to change. When you realize your own helplessness in a particular situation, when you give up your belief in your own strength, then God has more room to act in your life—and your belief in Him will intensify and stretch.

God of mercy, I realize I am helpless to control all the circumstances in my life. I believe in Your love, and I want to give You the space You need to enter my thoughts, my emotions, and each and every situation in my life.

Are You Gullible?

The gullible believe anything they're told;
the prudent sift and weigh every word.
PROVERBS 14:15 MSG

Buy this diet product and you'll lose twenty pounds. Drink this soda and life will be more fun. Splash on this perfume and romance will be yours. Invest in this program and your savings will double. Apply this face cream and you'll look twenty years younger. Commercials have tremendous power to shape your beliefs. But the wise author of Proverbs 14:15 has good advice for you: don't fall victim to false promises. Before you believe something, ask questions, research your options, sift through the facts. The Hebrew word that's been translated here as "believe" has these additional meanings: security, sureness, nourishment, stability, truth. Be careful where you look for these things; be careful what you choose to believe. Belief in God's promises will never let you down.

Remind me, Lord of truth, to be careful about what I believe.
May Your love be the standard against which I measure my beliefs.

Belief and Your Emotions

"The Lord himself goes before you and will be with you; he will never leave you nor forsake you. Do not be afraid; do not be discouraged."
DEUTERONOMY 31:8 NIV

Where do your beliefs come from? Do they depend on your emotional reactions to whatever is going on around you? We all tend to perceive life through our emotions, but in reality, they are as limited as our physical vision. The world we see with our eyes is only a piece of reality, a glimpse into an enormous and mysterious universe. Just as our eyes often deceive us, so do our feelings. This means that whether you sense God's presence or not, He is always with you. On the days when you are sad and discouraged, He is just as close to you as He is on the days when you are happy and confident. God's grace is with you right now, in this moment, and it also waits for you in the future. Disregard your feelings of fear and discouragement. Don't let your emotions dictate your beliefs. Believe in God's love!

Lord, when my belief in You wavers, remind me that You never change. No discouragement or fear of mine can ever limit Your love.

A Wonderful Promise

*"Whatever you ask for in prayer, believe that you
have received it, and it will be yours."*
MARK 11:24 NIV

This is a wonderful promise Jesus made to us—but it's also hard to know what to do with it. How can we believe in something that's just not there? And if our belief is too weak, will God punish us by withholding the thing we're praying for? Is it the power of our belief that shapes God's ability to answer prayer? Should we try to "work up" more belief so we can get the thing we want?

Questions like these are natural ones, but they come from thinking with a human perspective rather than God's. Prayer is not about getting what we want; it's not meant to satisfy our egotistical and selfish desires. Instead, prayer is about spending time with God; it's about opening our hearts to His Spirit so that He can begin to shape our beliefs and desires. His power and ability to act do not depend on anything we can "work up," only on our surrender to His love.

*Spirit of love, I believe in You. I believe You have the power to work in
my life. I ask that You shape my longings and give wisdom to my prayers.
May my prayers and the desires of my heart lead me ever closer to You.*

Belief and Hope

I pray that God, the source of hope, will fill you completely with joy and peace because you trust in him. Then you will overflow with confident hope through the power of the Holy Spirit.
ROMANS 15:13 NLT

We tend to think of hope as a cheery, optimistic outlook on life—but the biblical concept of hope goes far deeper and has wider consequences. Biblical hope is the confident expectation that God will do amazing things in the future; it's the belief that the same God who was with us yesterday will be with us tomorrow. When we lose this confidence, that's when things seem hopeless. We feel as though the future is empty and barren. But hopelessness is a lie, for God always has big plans for us! Belief in His promises is the foundation for a life of hope, a life of joy, a life of peace.

Source of hope, I believe You have an amazing future planned for me. I am confident Your Spirit is working out everything, creating for me a life of peace and joy.

The Prince of Peace

For unto us a child is born, unto us a son is given. . .
and his name shall be called. . .The Prince of Peace.
ISAIAH 9:6 KJV

You may be familiar with this verse from the prophet Isaiah because it is sung in Handel's *Messiah*. If so, you may connect the words with Christmas: the birth of the Christ child who was the Prince of peace. Belief in the Prince of Peace, however, offers blessings all year round. God wants you to experience the Christ child's peace not just as a Christmas card wish for the month of December but in your ordinary, everyday life, twelve months a year.

The Hebrew word translated "peace" is *shalom*, a word with many shades of meaning that include completeness, prosperity, safety, contentment, health, rest, comfort, ease, and wholeness. If you believe in the Prince of Peace, you can trust He will lead you along paths to comfort and contentment; He will work to make you whole and healthy, safe and sound. You can relax, even on your most stressful days, knowing you're relying on Christ's shalom at work in your heart and life.

Prince of Peace, even in a world of conflict and tension,
I believe in Your shalom. Bring comfort, completeness,
safety, and wholeness to the world—and to my heart.

Believe in Christ's Peace!

Jesus said, "Put your sword back where it belongs.
All who use swords are destroyed by swords."
MATTHEW 26:52 MSG

By the standards of many people today, Peter would have been perfectly justified in using his sword to defend Jesus. But Christ has a different standard. He asks that we believe in His call to peace, even as the world's violence bombards us from all directions. It comes at us on the news, in movies, and on TV. It invades our schools and our workplaces. We see it on our highways, on city streets; sometimes it even invades our homes. We may think we have no part in the world's violence, but Jesus calls us to examine our hearts. In the Gospels, He said that if our thoughts are full of rage and hatred, then we too nurse the roots of violence. What's more, violence harms both the victim and the one who does the violence. Even if we think we are protecting ourselves, we need to ask ourselves if we aren't actually believing in the old rule of an eye for an eye and a tooth for a tooth. Jesus put an end to that rule, and now He asks us to believe in His new rule of love and compassion. He wants us to be His hands and feet on this earth, spreading peace instead of violence.

Jesus, may I not wield the sword of violence against anyone,
even within my heart. I believe in Your rule of peace, and I
ask that You use me to build a world of love and safety.

Clothed in Belief

She is clothed with strength and dignity,
and she laughs without fear of the future.
PROVERBS 31:25 NLT

The woman in Proverbs 31 believed in God's promises. She clothed herself in them as though they were her finest robes. They gave her strength, dignity, beauty, and a sense of security. They allowed her to look into the unknown and smile with the same playful anticipation a child feels on Christmas Eve. When the Proverbs 31 woman laughed at the future, she wasn't pretending that troubles and challenges didn't lie ahead. She knew that sooner or later she would face the loss of loved ones, and the day of her own death would one day arrive. But those realities did not shake her belief in God. She could joke at her fears for the future, not because she was hiding her head in the sand, but because she was confident that God's love was the foundation of each thing she would experience, including death. When we share her belief, we too no longer have to fear the future; we can even face death with a smile of anticipation.

Lord of both life and death, I ask that You give me the strong belief of the woman in Proverbs 31. May that belief be the clothing I wear each day as I head out into the world, so that I may look into the future and laugh with joy, knowing You have infinite blessings in store for me.

Belief That Leads to Health and Peace

A peaceful heart leads to a healthy body; jealousy is like cancer in the bones.
PROVERBS 14:30 NLT

Our beliefs about our emotions are powerful, and those beliefs inflate the power of our emotions even more. Believing that a bad mood is something we have no control over, we may snap at our loved ones, using our emotional misery as an excuse for the pain we cause. Or we may be so convinced by the worry or jealousy we're experiencing that we begin to distrust God's promises of blessing and plenty. When that's the case, we need to replace our beliefs about our emotions with this wisdom from Proverbs, which tells us that some emotions are meant to be nourished—and others need to be quickly dropped into God's hands.

Learn to cultivate and seek out what brings peace to your heart. Practice letting go of your negative feelings as quickly as you can, releasing them to God. Don't believe in their power! No emotion is a sin; but if you cling to your dark feelings, they can reproduce like a cancer, blocking the healthy flow of God's blessings into your life.

I believe You are more real, more powerful, more certain than my emotions, Lord. May I rely on Your Word rather than my feelings.

Lose Your Life?

"For whoever wants to save their life will lose it,
but whoever loses their life for me will save it."
LUKE 9:24 NIV

Life is full of paradoxes. God seems to delight in turning our ideas inside out and backward, and again and again, we come across scriptures that seem hard to believe. This verse is a good example. It doesn't seem to make sense—and yet we can believe its truth. The more we try to cling to people and possessions, the emptier our lives end up being. The only way to possess our life is to surrender it absolutely into God's hands. As we let go of everything, God's grace gives everything back to us, transformed by His love.

Lord of paradox, I believe Your Word even when it's hard to
understand. Your love turns my reality inside out: when I lose
my life, You give it back to me; when I let go of my need to be
in control, You give me true freedom; and when I release my
grasp on my belongings, You bless me with everything I need.

Light!

"If you are filled with light, with no dark corners, then your whole life will be radiant, as though a floodlight were filling you with light."
LUKE 11:36 NLT

We like to believe we can hide parts of ourselves where no one will see them: out of sight, out of mind. We hide them from others; we hide them from ourselves; we even try to hide them from God. We somehow convince ourselves that what we refuse to look at doesn't exist. But those hidden things don't go away. No matter what we believe, they still have the power to hurt us and others. Meanwhile, God wants to shine His light into even our darkest, most private nooks and crannies. He wants us to step out into the floodlight of His love—and then believe that His love will make us shine.

God of light, I believe You can make me shine. I ask You to reveal anything I've kept hidden, even from myself, so that I can be radiant with Your love.

Trained by Trouble

No discipline seems pleasant at the time, but painful.
Later on, however, it produces a harvest of righteousness
and peace for those who have been trained by it.
HEBREWS 12:11 NIV

Sometimes life just seems to wear us down. We can usually cope with the endless mini crises that fill our lives, but eventually, sooner or later, we all reach a point where we start to believe we've had all we can take. Giving up seems like the only option. It may be some small event that tips us over from belief in God's promises to fear and doubt—or it may be a major life change, an illness or the death of a close friend or loved one. Whatever it is, it's the last straw. Life just doesn't make sense anymore.

God never wants you to feel unnecessary pain, and His heart aches for you when your belief in Him is shaken. But He also wants you to learn that He can use even the hard things in life to draw you closer to Him. He is training you to trust Him, absolutely and totally.

Train me, God, to trust You more. May my belief in You
remain firm, even in the midst of crisis and challenge.

Worry and Belief

"Do not worry about tomorrow, for tomorrow will worry about its own things. Sufficient for the day is its own trouble."
MATTHEW 6:34 NKJV

All of us worry. We worry about the future. We worry about our finances. We worry about our family. We worry about work responsibilities. The list of worries is endless. Worry begins to feel like a normal state of mind for many of us—but in reality, worry robs us of our belief in God's unending care. Psychologists reinforce Jesus' message, telling us that worry is the fear of things that aren't currently real (and may *never* be real); it's the belief in a make-believe future conjured up by our fearful minds.

The root word for the English *worry* is an Old German word that meant "to strangle"—and worry truly has the power to strangle our spiritual lives. Worry makes it so we can't breathe in the Spirit of God. It twists our beliefs and interferes with the flow of God's life into ours. But our worries can be turned into prayers. Each time a worry pops into our heads, we can lift it up to God. As we offer our worries to Him, they will loosen their stranglehold on our lives. And then we will find ourselves once more believing in all God promises.

Jesus, I believe Your promises to me. When worries threaten to overwhelm me, teach me to replace each anxious thought with one of the promises You have given me.

Belief and Relaxation

*"First pay attention to me, and then relax.
Now you can take it easy—you're in good hands."*
PROVERBS 1:33 MSG

Maybe you believe you need to be on constant alert in order to deal with your life's many challenges. While being alert is a good quality, one that can prevent you from overlooking important clues about yourself and others, it can all too easily turn into an unhealthy tension, a state of constant stress as you struggle to be ready for each day's problems and dilemmas. This stress stems from the belief that everything is up to you; deep in your heart, you believe the world really *could* end if you fail to keep up with your responsibilities. This kind of thinking robs you of your joy. What's more, it's based on faulty thinking. When you believe God has everything under control, you can relax. Go with the flow. Focus your attention on God—and He will give you exactly what you need to handle each moment of every day.

*God of constant care, I believe You have my life in Your
hands. Take my stress and replace it with the joy of Your
presence. Give me greater confidence in You so that I can
relax and release my tension into Your loving hands.*

Beliefs about Food

He gives food to every living thing. His faithful love endures forever.
PSALM 136:25 NLT

As women, we often have confused beliefs about food. Many of these false beliefs come from our society, which is also confused about food. We love to eat—but we feel guilty when we do. We sometimes turn to food when we're tense or worried, trying to fill the empty, anxious holes in our hearts. The comfort that food gives us is short-lived, though, because then we beat ourselves up for overeating and end up feeling worse than we did before.

God wants us to have healthy beliefs about food. Food is one of God's blessings; at the Last Supper, Jesus even used food to represent His own body. As our beliefs about food become rooted in a healthier, more biblical perspective, God will bless us with the true nourishment we need, both body and soul.

Jesus, I ask You to heal any unhealthy beliefs I have about food. May I remember You each time I eat.

World-Changing Love

Let all that you do be done in love.
1 CORINTHIANS 16:14 NRSV

What do you believe about love? If you're like most of us, you have conflicting beliefs. Our world isn't too clear on what the definition of love actually is. Sometimes our beliefs limit the power love has to change the world, especially if we think love is only an emotion. The Bible teaches us that love is more than a feeling; it needs to become real through action. We grow in love as we act in love. Some days, the emotion may overwhelm us; other days, we may feel nothing at all. But if we express our love while making meals, driving the car, talking to our friends and families, or doing our work, God's love will flow through us to those around us. Our belief in the power of love will grow wider and deeper.

God of love, I believe Your love is the most powerful thing in the world. I ask that You remind me to never limit Your love with beliefs that diminish its power and reality. May everything I do and say be an expression of Your miraculous, world-changing love.

Belief to Make You Thrive

Those who trust in their riches will fall,
but the righteous will thrive like a green leaf.
PROVERBS 11:28 NIV

Most of us believe money is pretty important. After all, so many things we want depend on having enough money—that remodeling project we're hoping for, the summer clothes we want to buy, the Christmas gifts we want to give, the vacation we hope to take, and the new car we want to drive. There's nothing wrong with any of those things, but our enjoyment of them will always be fleeting. That's why we need to take a good look at what our beliefs really are. Deep down, do we believe money can make us happier than God can? False beliefs like that get us off track. But as we place our beliefs on God's promises, His blessings make us truly grow and thrive.

God of abundance, reveal to me the false beliefs I'm
harboring in my mind. Show me how to let them go. I know
that money can never make me thrive the way You can.

Belief in God's Presence

"If you seek him, you will find him."
1 Chronicles 28:9 NLT

What do you believe about prayer? Do you know if your beliefs line up with scripture? The Bible doesn't say you have to pray in a particular way in order to find God. It doesn't tell you to follow an elaborate prayer discipline or practice specific techniques. Certain disciplines can be helpful to your spiritual life, but when it comes right down to it, the Bible makes clear that prayer is very simple: all you have to do is look for God—and whether you sense His presence with you or not, you can be confident He is with you. The very act of turning toward God, believing in His potential and power, is the most basic and effective form of prayer. The moment you cry out to God, "Help!" you acknowledge that your own strength is not enough, that you're willing to let go of your control of your life and believe in God's love and power. God doesn't need a special signal from you to get His attention. He's always there, ready to listen, ready to help.

God of power and love, I believe You are always with me, always waiting to bless me, and always willing to help me, no matter what my need is. Thank You for Your constant presence in my life.

Belief in Yourself

To get wisdom is to love oneself; to keep understanding is to prosper.
PROVERBS 19:8 NRSV

The author of Proverbs 19:8 has wise advice for you. His voice comes to you across the millennia, assuring you that wisdom and understanding go hand in hand with self-respect. God wants you to have healthy self-love. In fact, false beliefs about your own unworthiness can actually get in the way of God's blessings. The kind of self-love the Bible talks about isn't arrogant or egotistical; it doesn't have anything to do with selfishness. Instead, if you believe in your own worth, you will find you are more able to be of use in God's kingdom. If you are patient with yourself, you are likely to be more tolerant of others as well. And if you have learned to forgive yourself, you will find you can more easily forgive someone else. So believe in yourself. Know that God loves you and has a purpose for your life. Use your abilities joyfully to serve God and those around you. Let go of any false beliefs about yourself that are interfering with God's blessing, and replace them with the sure knowledge that you are worthy of respect and care.

Wise Lord, I believe You created me to be a strong woman, beautiful inside and out. My God-given identity deserves my care and respect. Banish the lies I've believed about myself, I pray, and replace them with Your love.

Believe in Rest!

If you sit down, you will not be afraid.
PROVERBS 3:24 NRSV

Have you ever asked yourself, *What beliefs about work and rest have I absorbed from my family and from the society I live in? Are these beliefs based on God's Word?* Many of us carry within our minds the belief that we must be constantly busy, that we should feel guilty for resting, that we need to push ourselves harder and harder. But the wise author of Proverbs 3:24 tells us we don't need to be afraid to sit down. Other Bible translations use the phrase "lie down," and the original Hebrew word has to do with rest, relaxation, even sleep.

God is happy when you take a break from your work and responsibilities. He calls you to come into His presence and simply sit and relax for a while. Human beings have limitations—physically, spiritually, and emotionally—and believing you have to be constantly busy denies these limitations. God alone has no limits. As you become rooted in healthy beliefs about who you are and who God is, you'll no longer hesitate to pause now and then for rejuvenation and rest.

God of rest, I believe that only You are limitless. Teach me to responsibly care for my own needs, including my need for relaxation.

Beliefs about Nourishment

"Give us today our daily bread."
MATTHEW 6:11 NIV

Sometimes, your beliefs about food, weight, and appearance get in the way of what God wants for you. Do you ever find yourself believing you *need* ice cream to make you happy? Or do you believe you're a better person if you constantly diet and deprive yourself of calories? Do you believe the number on your scales determines your worth? Or do you believe you have to conform to a Barbie doll ideal for your weight and appearance? All these misguided beliefs—all of which you absorb from the world around you—deny the reality: God wants to bless your body as much as He wants to bless your soul. Like a loving mother, He delights in your daily nourishment. Your body needs healthy food as much as your soul needs prayer and quiet. God knows what you need each day to thrive and grow.

Jesus, thank You for the prayer You gave us in the Gospels.
Remind me to shape my beliefs around Your words,
rather than the world's attitudes and values.

Belief in God's Bounty

Oh, the depth of the riches of the wisdom and knowledge of God!
How unsearchable his judgments, and his paths beyond tracing out!
ROMANS 11:33 NIV

Money is the way our culture measures value, but we forget that it's just a symbol, a unit of measurement that can never span the infinite value of God's love and blessing. Imagine trying to use a tape measure to stretch across the galaxy, or a teaspoon to determine how much water is in the sea. In the same way, it simply doesn't make sense to believe money can measure the reality God offers us.

Don't let your beliefs about money limit your perception of the amazing life God has given you. See past the world's misconceptions. Believe in the unknowable depth and breadth of divine grace!

Bountiful Lord, I believe Your abundance is so great that no dollar amount could ever define it. Teach me to look at my life with kingdom eyes, rather than the world's eyes, so that I can begin to see as You see.

Outbursts of Love

Think of ways to motivate one another to acts of love and good works.
HEBREWS 10:24 NLT

What are the beliefs that define the beginning of your day? Do you believe God has something amazing in store for you in the next twelve hours—or do you believe the day ahead will be dreary and boring? Your beliefs about the day will shape what you experience, and they may also shape the experiences of those around you. Our beliefs are contagious!

Now, imagine you're sitting in the bleachers watching one of your favorite young people play a sport. You leap up and cheer for her; you make sure she knows you're there, shouting out encouragement. Hearing your voice, she jumps higher, runs faster. Your excitement spurs her on. That's the same sort of excitement that comes to life when you believe God is waiting to bless you each day. That excitement will spread to those around you, encouraging them as well. And as your beliefs change, pay attention. You may notice love and kindness bursting out into the world in surprising ways!

I believe You have something marvelous in store for me today, Lord. Keep my eyes open to see Your blessings, and may the excitement and anticipation I feel today spread to those I meet. May Your love burst out from me!

Guilt and Shame

*Once you were far away from God, but now you have been
brought near to him through the blood of Christ.*
EPHESIANS 2:13 NLT

Do you ever believe the wrong choices you've made have separated you from God? Does your sense of guilt or shame create a barrier that prevents you from believing in the power of God's promises?

Psychologists say that guilt can be a healthy emotion, one that drives us to make positive changes in our lives. Shame, on the other hand, is toxic. Instead of pushing us to become better people, it over and over tells us the lie that we are bad, worthless, ugly. So take a look at your beliefs about the mistakes you have made. Do you believe they are so great you can never be redeemed, never claim your birthright as a child of God? Or do you believe Jesus has the power to heal you? Are you confident that the creative force of God's love can help you grow into the person you were always meant to be?

*Jesus, I believe Your life and death make all the difference
in my own life. I can bring my guilt to You, and You will wash
me and heal me. Remove any shame from my heart, I pray,
so that I can believe the truth of Your love for me.*

Don't Believe the Perfection Lie!

The LORD directs our steps, so why try to understand everything along the way?
PROVERBS 20:24 NLT

As women, many of us were taught that "good enough" means perfection. We absorbed the idea that we need to make everyone happy, all the time, and we need to do it *perfectly*. Of course, none of us can live up to that standard. That doesn't stop us from trying, but we end up feeling frustrated, ashamed, confused, overwhelmed, and exhausted.

Perfectionism and the need to please are based on false beliefs. When you replace them with the beliefs that God is moving in your life, that He is in control, and that His strength and love are working through you, you can begin to relax. God knows your desire to love others, to serve, and to make wise choices. He hears your prayers for help and strength. Now believe His promises. Lean back and take a deep breath. The Creator of the universe is directing your steps—and He knows what He's doing!

*Creator God, I believe You are working in my life. Even when
I don't understand what's happening, I believe You have
a plan and a purpose You are bringing to fulfillment.*

Belief and Gratitude

*God is able to bless you abundantly, so that in all things at all times,
having all that you need, you will abound in every good work.*
2 CORINTHIANS 9:8 NIV

How often do you take time to reflect on the blessings in your life? If you're honest, you may have to admit that your attention tends to focus on all that is wrong with your life, instead of all that is right. But to be truly healthy and happy, you need to have a grateful heart. Gratitude bolsters your belief in God.

In a recent study, two psychologists tested the value of "counting our blessings." They asked three groups of students to respond to a weekly questionnaire for ten weeks. The first group listed five things they were grateful for each week, the second group listed five problems they'd had in the past week, and the third group simply wrote down five "events or circumstances" from the past week. Know what the psychologists discovered? At the end of the ten weeks, the students in the "gratitude group" were not only emotionally happier but also physically healthier. They reported that they had more energy for exercise, they got more sleep, and they felt more rested when they got up.

In other words, we are blessed by counting our blessings!

*God of blessing, I believe You fill my life with good things,
every day. Remind me that gratitude helps me see Your truth—
and in seeing and believing, I am still more blessed.*

Confident Belief

The LORD will be your confidence and will keep your foot from being caught.
PROVERBS 3:26 NRSV

Life is full of change. With each new change comes adventure, fulfillment, and excitement—but also fear and uncertainty. As you head into some new challenge, check your beliefs. They may be holding you back and undermining your confidence as you venture forth. If you believe that something is too much for you to handle, that belief can trip you up and make you fall.

For example, are you starting a career and overwhelmed with all you must learn? Are you a new mother, wondering if you'll be able to raise this tiny person who is depending on you so completely? Have you noticed that your marriage relationship has changed—and you're not sure what to do about it? Or are you facing new decisions and challenges now that you're a single woman again, due to divorce or widowhood? Whatever stage of life you're in and whatever particular changes you're currently facing, have confidence in God. Believe He is all you need—and you can head into new experiences with your heart at peace. Never fear: He will keep you from falling flat on your face!

Lord, thank You that You never change, no matter how much life may change around me. I believe You are the Rock that holds me steady. You are my anchor in the midst of wild seas. I have confidence in You!

Kindness

Your own soul is nourished when you are kind.
PROVERBS 11:17 TLB

We live in a society that all too often believes in a dog-eat-dog reality. The person who pushes hardest gets ahead, and my needs are always more important than yours. But the Bible asks us to examine those beliefs and realize they're not in line with God's rule of love. The world God created is interconnected at so many levels that I can't hurt you without hurting myself—and when I'm kind to you, my own soul is nourished.

If I'm harsh with myself, constantly criticizing myself, I'll find it harder to be kind to you. The lies I believe about myself will hold me back from reaching out to you in love. Kindness is an attitude that's built on belief in God's love. As we demonstrate our belief through acts of kindness, both to ourselves and to others, we flourish and grow. We are nourished. We are blessed.

God, I believe Your rule of love is at the heart of all creation. May I demonstrate Your love by being kind, to myself as well as to those around me.

Daily Miracles

"That is why I tell you not to worry about everyday life—whether you have enough food and drink, or enough clothes to wear. Isn't life more than food, and your body more than clothing?"
MATTHEW 6:25 NLT

With our eyes fixed on what we *don't* have, we often overlook the blessings we have already received. We believe we need more and more and more in order to be happy; meanwhile, God has blessed us in so many ways we often ignore. Think about it. Your body functions day after day in amazing ways you probably take for granted—your eyes taking in sights, your fingers feeling textures and temperatures, your ears hearing, your nose smelling, your mouth tasting. Inside your body, your heart beats steadily, moment after moment; your digestive processes do their work to break down food and provide nourishment to your cells; and the neurons in your brain and spinal cord fire endlessly, allowing you to think and move. Every cell of your body is busy with the life God gave you. When you look at the world around you with your spiritual eyes open wide, you'll also notice an abundance of daily miracles—from the love of friends and family to the smile of a stranger.

So why do we worry so much about material things, when we live in such a vast sea of daily blessing?

Generous Lord, I surrender to You my belief that I need more of everything in order to be happy. I believe You bless me daily with everything I need to live and thrive.

Believe in Love!

May the Lord make your love for one another and for all people grow and overflow, just as our love for you overflows.
1 Thessalonians 3:12 NLT

As a very young child, you believed you were the center of the world. As you grew older, you had to go through the painful process of learning that others' feelings were as important as yours. God wants to lift your perspective even higher now. He wants you to overflow with love for other people. He yearns for you to believe, deep down, that everyone is worthy of love—and then He asks that you be willing to demonstrate that love to every person you encounter, regardless of their appearance, their beliefs, their gender or race, or their irritating habits. Love isn't always easy. But with God's grace, as you allow His Spirit to take up more and more room in your heart and mind, love will fill you up and overflow out into the world around you.

Dear Lord, I believe You are love. I want to be filled with You—so that means I need to be filled with love. Point out to me any beliefs I have that would limit the flow of Your love through me.

Beliefs about the Past

"All their past sins will be forgotten, and they will live because of the righteous things they have done."
ᴇᴢᴇᴋɪᴇʟ 18:22 ɴʟᴛ

Do you believe you can't do anything about the past? Do you believe all your mistakes are back there behind you, carved in stone for all eternity? God wants to wipe away that belief. His creative power is amazing, and His grace can heal even the past. As you place your confidence in His love, yesterday's sins will be pulled out like weeds, while the good things you have done will be watered so that they grow and flourish into the present. Give your past to God. Believe that His grace is big enough to heal even your greatest mistakes and your worst memories.

God of grace, I believe not only that You have forgiven my past failures but that Your creative love is strong enough to heal the past so that I can thrive in the present and on into the future. May nothing from my past keep me from becoming all You have called me to be.

Steadfast and Secure

They will have no fear of bad news; their hearts are steadfast,
trusting in the LORD. Their hearts are secure, they will have no fear.
PSALM 112:7–8 NIV

If you're like most of us, you fear bad news. You dread the sound of the phone ringing in the middle of the night. You may tense up when you hear an ambulance's siren—you worry for your loved ones' safety, your heart pounds, and adrenaline flows through your body. It's hard to control these natural reactions. Our bodies automatically respond to the threat of danger.

But the psalmist tells us that the secret to coping with life's bad news is the steadfast and secure heart that comes from believing in the Lord's promises. God can keep your mind and body from being swept away in a tide of fear and adrenaline. Prayer is the anchor that can hold you steady, tying you to God, who is unshakable. Whenever you feel the slightest nibble of anxiety, immediately turn your thoughts to God. Don't waste time worrying, letting your fear build up in your heart, mind, and body. Instead, make prayer your constant habit. Keep the anchor of your life safe and secure in the sea of God's love.

I believe, God, that You can hold me steady, no matter what
happens. When fears and anxiety fill my mind, remind me to
turn to You, knowing that Your love keeps my life secure.

Facing the Day

*She gets up before dawn to prepare breakfast
for her household and plan the day's work.*
PROVERBS 31:15 NLT

If you're like most women, you've got a lot to do. Each of your roles shouts for attention. Some days you wonder, *How can I do it all?* There just aren't enough hours in a day—which means you *can't* do it all. No one can. No matter how strong and capable you are, you have physical, emotional, spiritual, and intellectual limitations.

Whenever you encounter a new challenge in your life—whether you're a newlywed, a new employee, a first-time mother, a start-up business owner, or heading back to school—you are bound to encounter huge learning curves. You'll need to make adjustments. You may need to wake up early in order to get the spiritual and physical nourishment you need, as well as to prepare your heart and mind for the day. Having a plan for the day will help you be more efficient. Believe in yourself. Believe God will help you through the day ahead. And then head confidently into your day, your head high.

God, when self-doubts begin to overwhelm me, I believe You have the answers I need. Remind me to take extra time to be with You so that I can have the spiritual strength and confidence I need to face each day.

The Center of Your Being

Above all else, guard your heart, for everything you do flows from it.
PROVERBS 4:23 NIV

The Hebrew word translated as "heart" in this verse doesn't refer to the physical organ in your chest, nor does it have as much to do with your emotions as it does your thoughts and mind. The Hebrew word—*leb*—includes these meanings: "center of your being, mind, attention, inner life, thoughts, will, knowledge, understanding." Your beliefs, your thoughts, your mental habits—all impact both your emotions and your actions. Psychologists have learned that as we intentionally shape our thoughts and beliefs, we can change our lives. Ancient scholars were also wise enough to understand that when we protect our minds—the things we pay attention to, the thoughts we allow to occupy us, and the beliefs we harbor—we are actually caring for our entire being, body, mind, and soul. Guarding our inner lives also has an effect on our actions that will impact the world around us. This means we are to be careful about the ideas and thoughts we allow into our heads. We don't mindlessly absorb beliefs from the internet and TV. We practice wise self-care so that we can be our best selves.

Lord of my life, I believe You want only the best for me. Make me more aware of the thoughts and beliefs I've been allowing to grow inside me. Help me exercise care and diligence as I guard my heart against anything that denies You and Your love.

Cups of Blessing

You serve me a six-course dinner right in front of my enemies.
You revive my drooping head; my cup brims with blessing.
Psalm 23:5 msg

At the end of a long day, do you ever feel weak and ravenous with hunger? You've gone too long without eating, and now your body demands food. You may find yourself snapping at your family; when your blood sugar is low, it's hard to be your best self!

We often do the same thing to our spirits, depriving them of the spiritual nourishment they need—and then we wonder why life seems so overwhelming. We can't be our best selves without spiritual nourishment, any more than we can without physical nourishment. But dinner is on the table, and God is waiting to revive us with platefuls of grace and cups brimming with blessings. So today, no matter what enemies you are facing—discouragement, doubt, criticism, failure—believe in God's nourishing love. He has what you need to give you fresh energy and stamina.

Lord, I believe You have the nourishment I need to be strong, steady, and kind, no matter what challenges I face. When I've gone too long without a spiritual "meal," remind me I need to take time to sit down with You.

Believe in the Future!

*I focus on this one thing: Forgetting the past
and looking forward to what lies ahead.*
PHILIPPIANS 3:13 NLT

Paul, who wrote the letter to the Philippians, had made his share of mistakes. As a devout Jew, he'd been so angry with the followers of Jesus that he persecuted them and even killed them. When he changed his ways and began to follow Christ, it must have been hard for him to put his guilt and bad reputation behind him. But if he hadn't—if he hadn't believed in the power of Christ's forgiveness and redemption—he would never have been able to go on to do the tremendous work for God's kingdom that he did.

God calls you to look forward rather than backward. He asks you to stop focusing on the past and, instead, believe in the possibility and potential the future holds. Like every other human being in the world, you have made mistakes; but God does not want you to dwell on them, wallowing in guilt and discouragement. He pleads with you to let go of the past, as Paul did, trusting Christ to deal with whatever it holds. Believe His grace is new each and every moment—and you will gain new energy for the journey that lies ahead.

*Jesus, I believe You have freed me from the past—from my mistakes,
from my old wounds, from all I did to hurt myself and others. Now
help me let go of everything that lies behind me, so that I can go
forward into the future with a light heart and a high head.*

God's Power vs. the World's

*Better to be patient than powerful; better to
have self-control than to conquer a city.*
PROVERBS 16:32 NLT

Our world values visible power. We believe that things like prestige and skill, wealth and influence, are what make us important. But God looks at things differently. From His perspective, the quiet, easily overlooked quality of patience is far more valuable than any worldly power. Patience makes room for others' needs and brokenness. Patience creates a space in our lives for God's love to stream through us to those around us.

So ask yourself: *What do I believe about power? Do I believe that money, reputation, and talent will give me power? Or do I believe that nothing is more powerful than love?* The kind of power that relies on the world's values tends to be impatient; it's in a hurry to earn more, do more, consume more, and it's easily irritated when anyone or anything slows it down. Meanwhile, the power of love is gentle, willing to wait, ready to go without.

Lord of love, I believe Your power is greater than anything the world can offer. Remind me not to absorb the world's beliefs. Give me the patience and self-control I need to practice love in all my interactions.

Walls

The rich think of their wealth as a strong defense;
they imagine it to be a high wall of safety.
PROVERBS 18:11 NLT

Many of us believe that enough money will make us safe from the world's dangers. In reality, though, the walls that money builds can't keep out heartbreak and sorrow—but they can come between our hearts and God.

What walls have you built between yourself and Jesus? Try making a list of each barrier you sense between you and the Lord of love. Your list may be long—or it may have only one item, but that one item may have created a wall that stands tall and impenetrable. Once you have your list, take it in prayer to Jesus. His love can knock down any wall, no matter how tall.

You may want to prayerfully burn your list to symbolize your belief in the reality of Christ's power. Or you might want to discuss the "walls" with a trusted friend or spiritual adviser; sometimes we believe more easily in God's grace when it's spoken to us with a human voice. Whatever action you choose to take, you can be confident that no wall can separate you from the love of God!

Jesus, I believe Your love is stronger than any of the
walls I've erected in my mind. Knock down the false
beliefs that come between Your heart and mine.

Politics

By the blessing of the upright a city is exalted.
PROVERBS 11:11 NRSV

The Hebrew word that is translated as "city" in this verse referred to a corporate body of human beings, an organized community. In today's world, we might use the term *politics* to refer to a similar concept. In reality, *politics* simply refers to organized groups of people getting along and sharing power. Politics shapes human lives—and as Christ's followers, we are called to do all we can to ensure justice for the poor and the oppressed.

It's easy to feel helpless, as though there's nothing you can do that will really change your community and nation. This verse promises, however, that you have the power to make a significant difference in your neighborhood, city, or country, and even the world. What you believe about life and how you express those beliefs, how you treat your neighbors and coworkers, when and how you speak up for justice and love—all have the power to reach further than you may realize. When you believe God's promises to use you for His kingdom, your life has the potential to bless the human community you live in.

God of justice, I ask You to remind me daily that what I say and do, the viewpoints I support, and the leaders I endorse all matter to You. Give me wisdom to see Your path through the confusing political arena. May I never forget love is always Your first priority.

Believing in What We Can't See

Now faith is being sure of what we hope for,
being convinced of what we do not see.
HEBREWS 11:1 NET

"Seeing is believing." This little saying has been around since at least the seventeenth century. But the Bible asks us to believe in what we *can't* see. This goes against our human nature. It's hard to believe in something when we've never seen it; and like children, we hate to wait for the physical evidence of God's blessings. We get impatient, and we forget that God sees from a perspective outside time. He plans to give us everything we need at exactly the right moment. While we wait on His timing, we need to cultivate a grateful heart for both the things that we have—and the things we are still waiting for. Gratitude will help us believe.

In the Hebrew scriptures, the Lord commanded the Israelites to count their harvest, beginning the day after the Sabbath during Passover (Leviticus 23:15). For nearly two thousand years, the Jewish people had no homeland, and they had no harvest to count—and yet they continued to obey this commandment. They counted a harvest that from the world's perspective simply didn't exist. But they counted it as an act of faith, a visible demonstration of their belief in God's promises. By comparison, how strong is *your* belief?

God, I do believe in You. I believe in Your promises. And yet some
days, I need to pray along with the man who came to Jesus,
"I do believe—but help my unbelief" (see Mark 9:24).

Wise Boundaries

"I, Wisdom, live together with good judgment. . . . I was there when [the Lord] set the limits of the seas, so they would not spread beyond their boundaries."
PROVERBS 8:12, 29 NLT

In Proverbs, Wisdom is personified as a woman. When God designed the world, Lady Wisdom watched with joy as He drew distinct boundaries around the oceans and seas to protect the rest of His creation from drowning. Wisdom understood that boundaries are necessary; they are there for our protection.

But many of us as women have a hard time with boundary setting. We feel guilty saying no, so we say yes until we're pushed past our strength and out of our comfort zones. We believe that boundaries are the same as walls, barriers that interfere with relationships; when in reality, boundaries foster healthy relationships as they guard our own well-being.

No one has the right to step over your boundary lines and take advantage of you. God wants you to believe that boundaries are a part of His plan for your life.

Loving Lord, remind me to follow Lady Wisdom's example and take delight in the boundaries of protection You have created for my life. I believe Your wisdom will lead me into healthier relationships at home, at work, and in my community.

Clearing the Air

The speech of a good person clears the air.
PROVERBS 10:32 MSG

Do you ever have a hard time speaking the truth? For many of us, the truth is hardest when we're afraid it will hurt people's feelings or make them not like us. We believe the old lie that, as women, we have to please everyone and make them happy always. Even though we've come a long way as women, these old beliefs can still hold us back from the full stature God wants for us.

Knowing when and how to speak the truth can be confusing, but one way you can discover how to speak wisely is to examine Jesus' communication style. What did He say to friends? To enemies? How did He initiate conversations? Jesus paid attention to each individual. He listened carefully to what people had to say. He didn't push Himself on anyone—but at the same time, He wasn't afraid to speak the truth. His straightforward responses led to greater clarity in the interaction. Not everyone was happy with what He had to say, but that never stopped Him from speaking the truth in love.

Jesus, I believe Your interactions are the model I need to follow. May I no longer be held back by my need to please or my fear of offending. Remind me that love and truth go hand in hand—and that both have the power to clear away confusion and misunderstanding.

Believe in Forgiveness!

"Forgive others, and you will be forgiven."
LUKE 6:37 NLT

As human beings, our attitude toward forgiveness is often limited by our beliefs. We believe that some people simply don't deserve our forgiveness. Some hurts that we've suffered, we believe, justify holding on to unforgiveness. We think we don't need to forgive until the other person has proven he's changed or convinced us that he's truly sorry—and maybe even then, we still believe we're entitled to withhold forgiveness.

Jesus, however, tells us that we are to forgive others so that we too can enter into God's forgiveness. The implication is that our unforgiveness could hold us back from receiving the blessings of forgiveness God wants to give to our own hearts. The English word *forgive* comes from very old words that meant "to give up completely and wholeheartedly." When we forgive others, we give up our selfish need to be right, to have our own way. In a similar way, the Greek word translated as "forgive" in this verse means "to release, to set free." God has set us free from our mistakes and failures—and now He asks us to forgive others in the same way. As we give ourselves wholeheartedly to the work of forgiveness, God gives Himself completely to us.

Jesus, I believe You are calling me to new levels of forgiveness in my life. Remind me not to confuse setting healthy boundaries with forgiveness; teach me to honor both myself and others, as I honor You.

Patient Persistence

Patient persistence pierces through indifference;
gentle speech breaks down rigid defenses.
PROVERBS 25:15 MSG

When we're in the middle of an argument, we often become fixated on winning. We turn conflicts into power struggles, and we want to come out the victor. By sheer force, if necessary, we want to shape other people to our will. We believe that winning will make us the better person.

But that's not the way God treats us. His grace is gentle and patient, rather than loud and forceful. He calls us to believe that love and gentleness matter more than winning any argument. He asks us to follow His example—and let His quiet grace speak through us, in His timing rather than ours. As we believe in His power and unconditional love, we can let go of our own need to be right.

I believe, Lord, that Your love needs to be the priority I set for my life.
Help me be persistent and patient—rather than irritable and pushy,
insisting on my own opinion. Teach me to be gentle rather than harsh.

Perfect Peace

You will keep in perfect peace all who trust in you,
all whose thoughts are fixed on you!
Isaiah 26:3 nlt

Peace seems so far away sometimes—far from the world's situation, far from our communities, and far from our own hearts. We respond to the circumstances around us with anxiety and fear, believing the dangers are insurmountable. We'd like to feel peace, but nothing we see tells us that peace is possible.

Peace, however, isn't an emotion we can work up in our own strength—and it doesn't depend on what we can see with our physical eyes. Instead, peace is one of the blessings God longs to give us as we begin to believe His promises. When peace seems impossible, all we need to do is focus our attention on Him rather than on the world around us. As we give Him all our worries, one by one, every day, He will do His part: He will keep our hearts at peace.

Jesus, I believe that You can fill my heart with Your peace. I believe that
Your peace has the power to change me. . .and to change the world.

Alert. . .Diligent. . .Grateful

Pray diligently. Stay alert, with your eyes wide open in gratitude.
Colossians 4:2 msg

Our beliefs about prayer are often in need of correction. We assume that prayer is a once-a-day thing, maybe even a once-a-week thing. We believe we need a special time and environment in order to truly pray. But prayer is not a *sometimes* thing, it's not a *Sunday* thing, and it's not a *once-in-a-while* thing. It's an *all-the-time* thing! We need to believe prayer is an essential aspect of our daily lives, moment by moment, so we learn to keep the lines of communication open between God and ourselves all through each day. This kind of prayer doesn't require a certain amount of time, a particular place, or special words; it occurs anytime and anyplace, and it doesn't necessarily need any words at all. This verse gives us a clue as to how this state of prayer can be possible: it requires both alert awareness and gratitude. As we pay diligent attention to each moment—rather than living somewhere distant in our heads, preoccupied with our plans and worries—we will begin to notice how constantly God is blessing us. Alert and diligent gratitude creates the space where prayer becomes a continual state of mind.

Lord, I believe my heart and Yours can be in constant communion. You know, though, how easily I'm distracted, so remind me throughout my day to open my heart and mind to You. Keep me alert. Help me be diligent. Fill my heart with gratitude for Your many blessings.

A God Who Listens and Loves

"His ears are open to their prayers."
1 PETER 3:12 NLT

In 2010, sociologists Paul Froese and Christopher Bader published a book that describes Americans' beliefs about God. Their study found that about a quarter of Americans believe in an authoritative God who watches us only so He can catch us messing up. Another quarter of Americans believe in a critical, distant God who is waiting to punish people after they die. A third group believes in a disengaged God who set the world in motion and from then on ignored His creation. Finally, the fourth group believes in a God who is ready to rescue humans from their problems and crises. The researchers discovered that people's beliefs about God also shaped their politics and their style of interacting with others.

Take a moment to consider your own beliefs about God. Do they match up with what the Bible says? Are they compatible with the life of Jesus, who came to show us God's nature in human form? The Bible's God is not distant; His ear is tuned to your voice, and He longs to bless you, not punish you. Believe in a God of love who is constantly involved in the world He created—and that belief will shape your life.

God, I believe You are love. As I spend time with You, getting to know You better, erase from my mind any false beliefs I have about You.

Planning Ahead

A prudent person foresees danger and takes precautions.
PROVERBS 22:3 NLT

Believing in God doesn't mean you can just throw caution to the wind and sail blithely through life without taking any care or precautions. God expects you to use your own intelligence and common sense. The Bible recommends planning ahead, even as you trust God with every outcome. Whether you're going back to school, purchasing a new home, getting married, starting your own business, struggling to determine the best care for your aging parents, or going to be a new mom, you'll want to ask intelligent questions and plan for your next steps. Seek the advice of trusted friends and experts, do plenty of reading on reputable websites and in well-researched books, make a plan—and then turn the results over to God. Believing in God means trusting Him as you use all your abilities to serve Him.

God, I believe You have a plan for my life. Guide me to helpful information that will enable me to make wise decisions.

Don't Take Your Belief for Granted!

Be alert and of sober mind so that you may pray.
1 PETER 4:7 NIV

The apostle Peter knew all too well that our selfish fears can come between God and us. Peter believed in Jesus, but that didn't keep him from denying his closest friend on the night before His death. That's why Peter advises us to be alert and sober minded; he knew how easily our belief in God can be shaken. From personal experience, Peter was well aware that when we let our selfish concerns become uppermost in our minds, we lose our ability to communicate with God. We're so busy—running errands, driving here and there, checking our email, making phone calls, multitasking—that it's easy to let our belief in God fall into the background of our thoughts. We feel the constant pressure to somehow keep up with careers and family life, not to mention the demands of friends, church, and community; and by comparison, our belief in God seems far less urgent. But if we follow Peter's advice, we'll clear our minds so we can focus on God. Even on our busiest days—*especially* on our busiest days—we need to pay attention so that our thoughts and actions line up with our belief in God.

Jesus, remind me not to take my belief in You for granted. Give me the self-discipline I need to pay attention to our relationship.

Let God Set Your Pace

One who moves too hurriedly misses the way.
PROVERBS 19:2 NRSV

We live in a world that believes *fast* is better. Every day, we're bombarded with messages that say: *Hurry. Go faster. Accomplish more. Multitask so you get more done. Time's a-wasting.* Countless books have been published that focus on time management and promise to tell us the secret of how to do things faster and more efficiently so we can fit more into each day. But the promises those books offer are a mirage, because there are still only twenty-four hours in a day—and we're still not superwomen.

In 2013, researchers at the University of Toronto found that America's "fast-food mindset"—an impatient, ultraefficient culture that prioritizes speed over other values—interferes with our ability to appreciate small moments of pleasure. "Undermining people's ability to derive pleasure from everyday joys," the study concluded, "could exert a significant long-term negative effect on people's happiness."

Millennia ago, the author of Proverbs 19:2 already knew that speed is not the answer. God is never in a hurry—and He doesn't want you to dash through life and lose your way. Instead, He wants you to slow down and believe He will bless you in each and every moment.

Whenever I believe I have to go faster and faster, remind me, Lord, that You want me to rest in Your presence, relying on You to set the pace of my life.

Believing in Forgiveness

"If you see your friend going wrong, correct him. If he responds, forgive him. Even if it's personal against you and repeated seven times through the day, and seven times he says, 'I'm sorry, I won't do it again,' forgive him."
LUKE 17:3–4 MSG

The number seven in the Bible has a meaning greater than a mere numerical value. It symbolizes completeness, fullness, even eternity. So when Jesus spoke of forgiving someone seven times, He was using heavenly arithmetic. He was telling us that forgiveness should have no ceiling it can't reach beyond.

As humans, however, we tend to believe that forgiveness has reasonable limits. A person who repeats the same offense over and over can't be very serious when he asks for forgiveness, we tell ourselves. That just seems to make sense. And it *does* make sense from a human perspective. But lucky for us, God isn't reasonable. He forgives our sins no matter how many times we repeat them. His forgiveness is full, complete, endless. And He asks us to extend His heavenly arithmetic to others' faults as well.

Jesus, I believe You have forgiven all my sins; I believe Your forgiveness is absolute, without limits. Teach me not to set limits on my own ability to forgive. Teach me to believe love is strong enough to cover every failure and injury.

Patience and Courage

Wait patiently for the LORD. Be brave and courageous.
Yes, wait patiently for the LORD.
PSALM 27:14 NLT

Patience is all about waiting things out. It's about holding on another moment longer. It means enduring hard times. As a younger person, you probably believed you couldn't possibly endure certain things—but the older you get, the more you realize that you *can*. If you just wait long enough, the tide always turns. Hold on. Be patient. Believe that in time your life will change. God will rescue you from today's circumstances—and that belief will empower you with both patience and courage.

Lord, strengthen my belief in Your power to save and help, so that I can have the patience and courage I need to endure my life's challenges.

Your Number One Job

Be agreeable, be sympathetic, be loving, be compassionate, be humble.
That goes for all of you, no exceptions. No retaliation. No sharp-tongued
sarcasm. Instead, bless—that's your job, to bless. You'll be a blessing
and also get a blessing. Whoever wants to embrace life and see the
day fill up with good, here's what you do: Say nothing evil or hurtful;
snub evil and cultivate good; run after peace for all you're worth.
1 PETER 3:8–11 MSG

What do you believe is your most important job in life? Maybe it's your profession, or your family, or your volunteer work. But the Bible asks that as you think about those things, you remember the most important job God has given you to do: to bless others. In these verses, Peter spells out exactly how you do that—by getting along with others, by loving others and having sympathy for their problems, by not being selfish or arrogant, by being kind and avoiding situations where tempers fly, by making sure that your words build up rather than tear down, and by forgiving rather than trying to get even. If you head out into each day believing that blessing others is your number one responsibility, that belief will shape your every action. You'll be a blessing to others; and in return, God will bless you.

Remind me, Jesus, that my priority in life should always
be to bless others with my words and actions. I believe
You want to use me to show others Your love.

The Power of Your Words

Wise words bring many benefits.
PROVERBS 12:14 NLT

Maybe you believe the things you say have very little importance in the grand scheme of things. If so, that belief might encourage you to be careless in your conversations. In reality, your words have power. They can tear down others, causing them to doubt themselves and God. Or your words can empower those around you with hope and a sense of their own potential. What you say makes a significant difference in others' lives, in ways you may never realize. Your wise encouragement, concerned questions, and loving instruction will bring blessing into the lives of those with whom you interact.

God, I believe You can use my words to bless each person I encounter today. I ask that You fill my conversations with Your love.

His Unfailing Love

I trust in your unfailing love; my heart rejoices in your salvation.
PSALM 13:5 NIV

Most of us, at one time or another, feel unloved. Sometimes, deep in our hearts, we don't believe we even deserve to be loved. God longs to convince us at the deepest, most intimate level of our inner selves that He loves us—eternally, unconditionally, and totally. The Bible repeats this message of love over and over, and yet we hesitate to believe it.

Love is the reason Jesus came to earth. Love was the message He brought to us from God. Not a generic, all-purpose sort of love, but a unique love for each one of us, specific to our own hearts. We are each called by name, treasured and cherished.

The love of God is written into your very being. It is the force that connects the molecules of your body. It flows through your blood and sings in the neurons of your brain. And you see His love everywhere you look, for His love is what holds the world together. Believe in God's unfailing love—and your heart will rejoice!

*God, I believe You love me. I believe my very existence
springs from Your creative love. Let no self-doubt
of mine interfere with the intimacy we share.*

Claim God's Promises

"Look, I've given you this land. Now go in and take it. It's the land GOD promised to give."
DEUTERONOMY 1:8 MSG

The Bible is full of God's promises to us—but sometimes, because we don't totally believe, we neglect to claim these promises as our own. We read them, we hear them in sermons, we may even have memorized them; and yet, deep in our hearts, we're not convinced. As a result, our lives are not as full and rich as God longs for them to be. We leave those promises lying on the table, unclaimed; meanwhile, we experience needless pain and anxiety.

God yearns to give you so many blessings. Go ahead and believe in His promises. Take the gifts He's offering you. Believe—and begin to live a life of deep, wide, and endless blessing.

God, thank You for all You give me and for all You have promised to give me. Let no disbelief of mine stand in the way of Your love having full power in my life.

Leaning on a Friend

*Two people are better off than one, for they can help each
other succeed. If one person falls, the other can reach out
and help. But someone who falls alone is in real trouble.*
ECCLESIASTES 4:9–10 NLT

Our society has deeply ingrained beliefs about independence and
self-sufficiency—and those beliefs can make it hard for us to accept
help from others. The Bible tells us over and over, though, that we
are interconnected. We need each other. We cannot stand alone.
And God uses our relationships with each other to speak to us and
comfort us.

Have you ever noticed that in the best friendships, you take turns
being needy? You're strong enough to help your friend one day—
and the next day, she's the one offering you comfort and help. Over
and over, God uses our friends to make His love real in our lives,
while He uses us to spread His love back to our friends. So stop
believing that the only way to succeed is by "standing on your own
two feet," and don't be afraid to lean on a friend.

*Beloved Friend, I believe You put my friends in my life to show me
Your love. Remind me not to be too proud or too independent to
accept the blessings You long to bestow on me through my friends.*

Believe in Now!

God says, "At just the right time, I heard you. On the day of salvation,
I helped you." Indeed, the "right time" is now. Today is the day of salvation.
2 Corinthians 6:2 nlt

Meditation and consciousness exercises seek to direct our attention to the present moment, but many of us have a hard time living there for very long. It's as though we don't believe *now* matters as much as *before* and *after*. Sometimes, we hang on to the past, unwilling to let it go. Other times, we long for some future pleasure, convinced we can never be happy until it's ours. But God wants us to believe in *now*, because this is always where He meets us—here, in the present moment. We don't need to waste our time looking over our shoulder at the past, and we can stop believing we need to reach some future moment before we truly attain all that God wants us to have. God is here—*now*. Today, this very moment, is full of His blessing.

Lord, I believe You are blessing me right now, this very instant.
Remind me not to miss out on Your blessings because I'm
focusing on the past or future instead of the here and now,
where You are always waiting to meet me and bless me.

Self-Doubt

She sets about her work vigorously; her arms are strong for her tasks.
PROVERBS 31:17 NIV

As authors Katty Kay and Claire Shipman interviewed some of the world's most influential and successful women, they noticed something odd: no matter how intelligent and talented these women obviously were, and no matter what they had objectively achieved, each of these women suffered from self-doubt. When Kay and Shipman decided to investigate further, they discovered that a vast gap separates the sexes when it comes to self-confidence. Compared with men, women don't consider themselves as ready for promotions, they predict they'll do worse on tests, and they tend to underestimate their abilities. Despite the progress women have made over the past century, Kay and Shipman concluded that today's women continue to face a crisis of confidence.

The woman described in Proverbs 31 has often been held up as a model for Christian women—but we don't always believe in the values this woman holds out to us. The Proverbs 31 woman is neither weak nor passive. She knows her own strengths, and she uses them efficiently and vigorously. She doesn't let self-doubt hold her back. She believes in herself.

God, I believe You have given me strengths and abilities You want me to use for Your kingdom. May my belief in You help me believe more in myself—so that self-doubt never gets in the way of me doing and being all You have called me to do and be.

God's Priority

Jesus said, "'Love the Lord your God with all your passion and prayer and intelligence.' This is the most important, the first on any list. But there is a second to set alongside it: 'Love others as well as you love yourself.'"
MATTHEW 22:37–39 MSG

Sometimes we believe God wants things from us that He never said He wanted. We think a certain kind of daily devotional practice is required, or we assume church has to be a priority in our lives. Spending time with God and His people *is* important—but it's important for our own spiritual well-being. God never said He needed us to do those things to make Him happy. He never said, "Thou shalt read one chapter of the Bible every day, and then thou shalt spend a half hour in prayer. And then on Sunday, thou shalt spend at least two hours in a church building." Once again, those things can be helpful to our own spiritual journeys—but Jesus made clear what God's priority really is, and it's very simple: love. Daily devotions and Sunday church services are only important if they help us to better love God and others (and even ourselves).

Jesus, I believe love is Your number one priority for my life. May I stop putting the cart before the horse, believing I can please You by doing "religious" things. Let Your love shine through everything I do.

Those in Need

She opens her arms to the poor and extends her hands to the needy.
PROVERBS 31:20 NIV

Family, home, job, church, friends, personal and spiritual development—our days are so busy that it's hard to make time for anything extra. We believe we honestly care about those in need, but we only have so much time, energy, and money to go around. We truly believe we're doing all we can. But the Proverbs 31 woman once again challenges us to reexamine our beliefs. This woman took care of her family and herself; she was no self-sacrificing doormat. But she believed she was strong enough and rich enough in God's blessings that she had enough to share.

No one can do everything, and God doesn't expect us to be superwomen. But He does ask that we believe He'll use us to help those who are in need. The "poor" may lack financial resources, but they may also lack attention, love, physical energy, or skills. Look around you. See the people God might be asking you to reach out and help. Believe you can make a difference in someone's life—and God will use you and bless you.

God, I believe You want to use me to be Your hands, feet, eyes, and mouth, spreading Your love and help to those who need it.

Believe in God's Abundance!

From his abundance we have all received one gracious blessing after another.
JOHN 1:16 NLT

Some people only exist. They go through their days with their eyes on the ground, plodding along as though life were an endurance test. They believe their lives are dull and hopeless.

When you feel like that (and we all do, at one time or another), learn to look up. Believe that God has good things He's longing to give you. Don't overlook the small joys and tiny blessings He is showering into your life. It's easy to be so focused on the big things—financial challenges, your health problems, your loved ones' issues—that you forget to notice the many small ways God shows His love. Each new sunrise, each good meal, each warm bath, each good night's sleep—all send you love messages from your Father.

Cultivate the belief that each day that comes is a brand-new present from God to be unwrapped with joy. Hold out your hands. Accept His abundant blessings.

Abundant God, I believe You have blessings in store for me today. May I not be so preoccupied with my problems that I fail to see the grace and love You shower down on me.

Believe in God's Plan!

Commit your works to the LORD, and your thoughts will be established.
PROVERBS 16:3 NKJV

When you don't understand what's happening in your life and you aren't certain what to do next, believe that God has a plan for your life. Give Him all the details. Consciously and prayerfully place in His hands every aspect of your life. Then take the next step you can see, even if it's only a very tiny step. Don't be paralyzed by fear. Do what is in front of you to do. Although you still don't know what your long-term future holds, walk through the doors of opportunity that open each day. In time, God will bring new clarity to your thoughts, and you'll be able to see the path ahead.

*Lord, no matter how confused and lost I feel, I believe You have
a plan for my life. Show me the small steps I can take next.
Bless me with the certainty that You are leading me.*

Salvation

Show us how much you love us, GOD! Give us the salvation we need!
PSALM 85:7 MSG

In some churches, salvation in Christ is believed to be a crisis moment, a turning point, a dramatic Saul-on-the-road-to-Damascus conversion. But that's not what everyone experiences. Even if you did have that kind of dramatic conversion experience, Jesus' salvation is a steady, ongoing thing. Christ works in your life day by day, healing you, transforming you, and creating new life in you. According to Merriam-Webster's dictionary, the word *salvation* comes from the same roots as "safe," "make whole," "keep healthy," "make entire and complete." This is the salvation Jesus offers you. This is why He came to earth and died on the cross, so that He could offer you this ongoing health, this constant safety, this spiritual and emotional wholeness. By His power, you become all you were created to be, whole and holy, sanctified and complete. You need salvation on many levels: spiritually, of course, but also at the ordinary, day-to-day level of your emotions, habits, and thoughts. Believe that Jesus is saving you, over and over, throughout every day!

Jesus, I believe in Your constant salvation. Thank You for blessing me with wholeness and health, safety and fulfillment.

The Desires of Your Heart

*Take delight in the L*ORD*, and he will give you your heart's desires.*
PSALM 37:4 NLT

What kind of God do you believe in? Is He loving and generous—or stingy and cruel? Do you ever feel as though He wants to deny you what you want, as though He's a tightfisted stepparent who takes pleasure in thwarting you? That image of God is a lie. God is the One who placed your heart's desires deep inside you. As you turn to Him, believing that He alone is the source of all true delight, He will grant you what your heart most truly craves. That's what His Word promises—and you can believe it!

I believe, Lord, that You gave me the desires I feel—the deepest and truest longings of my heart—and I believe that You didn't give me these yearnings to tease me or torture me. Thank You that in Your time and in Your way, as I find my delight in You, You will give me the fulfillment I crave.

Believe in the Still Point!

*For Jesus doesn't change—yesterday, today,
tomorrow, he's always totally himself.*
HEBREWS 13:8 MSG

In one of T. S. Eliot's poems, he speaks of the "still point of the turning world." This is a place of stability and certainty, a place where our souls can find a sense of stillness and peace, even as the world continues to change around us. Meanwhile, of course, as human beings we continue to live in the stream of time. Sometimes all the changes that time brings terrify us; sometimes they fill us with joy and excitement. Either way, we can believe in that still point: Jesus Christ, who never changes. His constant, steady grace leads us through all life's changes; and one day, it will bring us to our home in heaven, beyond time.

*Jesus, I believe You are the constant center of all life. When life is
a whirl of change and challenge, I believe You will hold me steady.*

Believe in God's Renewal!

Take on an entirely new way of life—a God-fashioned life, a life renewed from the inside and working itself into your conduct as God accurately reproduces his character in you.
EPHESIANS 4:24 MSG

Life is full of irritations and stress. Bills to pay, errands to run, arguments to settle, endless responsibilities—they all rub at our hearts until we feel old and worn. At the end of a long week, we sometimes feel tired and drained, as though all our creativity and energy has been robbed from us. Instead of believing the lies that exhaustion tells us, we need to use those feelings as wake-up calls, reminders that we need to open ourselves anew to God's Spirit so that He can renew us from the inside out. God's love has the power to change our hearts and minds, filling us with new energy to follow Jesus. God will renew us. Day after day, over and over, as we believe in His promises, His blessing comes to us—making our hearts fresh and green, giving our minds and bodies new energy.

Creative God, I believe Your energy has the power to renew me—body, mind, and spirit.

Open the Curtains!

*But whenever someone turns to the Lord, the veil is taken away. . . .
So all of us who have had that veil removed can see and reflect the
glory of the Lord. And the Lord—who is the Spirit—makes us more
and more like him as we are changed into his glorious image.*

2 Corinthians 3:16, 18 nlt

Do you ever feel as though a thick, dark curtain hangs between you and God, hiding Him from your sight? Everyone has that feeling sometimes—but that's all it is: a feeling. It's not reality. We can still believe that the Spirit of God is with us, despite our feelings. The Bible says that all we have to do is turn our hearts to the Lord, and that sense of a curtain between us will be drawn back, letting God's glory and grace shine into our lives. When that happens, we can soak up the light, allowing it to renew our hearts and minds and mold us into the image of Christ.

*Spirit, I believe You are always with me, even when I
can't see You or sense Your presence. Remind me to turn
back to You again and again throughout my day.*

A Mother's Love

*I've cultivated a quiet heart. Like a baby content
in its mother's arms, my soul is a baby content.*
PSALM 131:2 MSG

A sleeping baby lies completely limp in her mother's arms, totally trusting and calm. No worries about the future disturb her peace. No anxiety makes her doubt her safety in her mother's arms. That's the attitude we all need to practice. It won't happen automatically; we need to constantly cultivate the belief that God holds us secure in His love. With that belief firm in our minds, we can let ourselves relax in God's arms, wrapped in His grace. Life will go on around us, with all its noise and turmoil, but we will be completely safe—totally secure, resting in trust.

*Loving Lord, I believe You love me with a mother's love. I believe I am
wrapped in Your arms, forever safe, no matter what is happening in the
world around me. Bless me, I pray, with peace and total confidence in You.*

Believe in the Lord's Care!

*"The LORD will guide you always; he will satisfy your needs in
a sun-scorched land and will strengthen your frame. You will be
like a well-watered garden, like a spring whose waters never fail."*
ISAIAH 58:11 NIV

What do you believe God wants for your life? This verse from
Isaiah tells you: God wants you to be healthy—not just physically,
but emotionally, intellectually, and spiritually as well. He wants to
fill your life with all the things you truly need. The life He wants
for you is not dry and empty and barren. Instead, it is lush and full
of delicious things to nourish you. Like everyone else in the world,
you'll have to cross life's deserts sometimes; but even then, you can
be confident that God will supply what you need to reach the next
oasis He has waiting.

*Shepherd of my heart, I believe You are always guiding me,
even when my life is challenging. I believe You will care for
me and nourish me, no matter the circumstances of my life.*

Goals

A longing fulfilled is a tree of life.
PROVERBS 13:12 NIV

In our hurry-up, goal-driven world, we often fail to take pleasure in the successes that come our way. Maybe we were longing to get our master's degree—but as soon as we got it, we instantly began longing for a better job. Or maybe we wanted a new house—and as soon as the papers were signed, we started planning a remodeling project. We thought we needed to be married in order to be happy—but once we were married, we believed we *had* to have children in order to find contentment.

Take stock of your life. What beliefs are shaping your attitudes about your achievements? Think about what you were most hoping to achieve a year ago, or five years ago. How many of those goals have you achieved? Don't move on too quickly from one goal to the next, never allowing yourself to find the blessing God wants to reveal in that achievement. With each goal reached, His blessing is spreading out into your life, like a tree whose branches grow ever wider.

I believe in the value of each of my life's achievements, Lord.
May I not discount or undervalue the goals You've helped me reach.

Open Communication

An open, face-to-face meeting results in peace.
PROVERBS 10:10 MSG

As women, many of us believe it's more loving to avoid honest communication than to share what we really feel, think, or need. Inside, we may be smoldering with resentment, but we keep those feelings hidden. Sometimes the resentment comes out anyway—not directly but "sideways," through passive-aggressive comments and actions. We believe people (especially our spouses!) should pick up on these hints we're giving about our state of mind, and then we become even more frustrated and resentful when our message isn't heard. This approach almost always fails to bring the results we desire.

We need to believe in our own right to have our feelings heard, honestly and openly. Sharing our complaints directly, without letting anger build up inside us, and encouraging others to do the same allows God's peace to flow into our relationships.

Lord, I believe You value my feelings and opinions. Help me value them too, while at the same time respecting others' feelings and opinions as well. Teach me to communicate more clearly, with respect for both myself and the other person. Bring Your peace to all my interactions.

The Invisible One

[Moses] kept right on going because he kept his eyes on the one who is invisible.
HEBREWS 11:27 NLT

You believe in God—but have you allowed your vision of Him to fade? In this life, you can't see God with your eyes, of course. Meanwhile, the physical world is right there in front of your nose: your family relationships, your household responsibilities, your job, your friends, your church—as well as the bills that keep arriving in the mail, the car that needs repairs, the furnace that is acting up, the roof that needs replacing, the child who is struggling at school, the arguments with your spouse that have been escalating lately, the tension between you and your mother. . . The list is endless, and all these things can very easily become more real to you than God is. Your belief in Him becomes an intellectual thing only, rather than an emotional and spiritual confidence that keeps you grounded through all life's challenges. Moses had plenty of those challenges as well, but he was able to keep going because his belief in the Invisible One was firm and steady.

God of Moses, I do believe in You—but sometimes, it's hard to see past the demands of the world around me. Give me sharper spiritual vision. May my belief in You give me the energy I need to keep going, no matter the challenges I face.

Life-Giving Words

A wholesome tongue is a tree of life, but perverseness in it breaks the spirit.
PROVERBS 15:4 NKJV

We've all heard the old saying "Sticks and stones may break my bones, but words will never hurt me." But do we believe it's true? The Bible says, no, it's not—and modern-day research shows that vicious teasing and persistent shaming and bullying lead to low self-esteem, depression, and even suicidal thoughts. On the flip side, encouraging, kind words not only heal and uplift but also cause a ripple effect, spreading out from seemingly unimportant conversations to bless situations and people we may never know of. Just as a well-watered tree produces nourishing fruit, we nurture others when we listen, reflect, and empower them with our words. That "fruit" will then go out into the world to bless others and grow new trees.

So believe in the positive power of your words!

Kind Lord, I believe You want my words to always reflect Your kindness. Guide my conversations, I pray, with Your Spirit of love.

Believe in Christ's Gift!

*For by grace are ye saved through faith;
and that not of yourselves: it is the gift of God.*
Ephesians 2:8 kjv

We live in a world that believes you can't get something for nothing. Everything comes back to "You scratch my back, I'll scratch yours." We learned that principle when we were very young—in the school cafeteria, maybe, when some little boy or girl said, "You give me your apple, and I'll give you my cookie." When we grew up, we understood that we wouldn't get far in life (or make any money) if we didn't work hard. We may have also learned that we have to earn others' respect and kindness with our own good behavior.

We tend to carry this understanding into our relationship with God. We believe we have to earn His favor—that He will only give to us if we give to Him. So we try to "be good." We follow all the rules. It's never good enough, of course. No matter how hard we try, we can never make ourselves good. But it doesn't matter! God turns our human rules upside down. He gives to us when we do absolutely nothing. He gives to us when we don't deserve anything. He gives to us no matter what.

Jesus, I believe I don't need to do anything to earn Your love. Thank You for the gift of Your life. Teach me to trust You more so that Your love can move through me and out into the world, unhindered by my doubts or disbelief.

Soak It In!

A good person basks in the delight of God.
PROVERBS 12:2 MSG

What do you believe about God's feelings toward you? Maybe you believe He loves you, but you still have the feeling, deep inside, that He basically just puts up with you. But the truth is God not only loves you—He also *likes* you!

Don't you love it when a friend says, "I had so much fun being with you"? You feel warm inside knowing that someone you like likes you back, that someone who gives you pleasure also gets pleasure from being with you. The Bible says God delights in you in a similar way. He loves to spend time with you. You make Him happy. Believe it or not—you are God's delight! Don't be afraid to bask in that knowledge, soaking it in like a cat soaking in the warmth by a fire.

Thank You, Lord, that You both love me and like me. When I begin to doubt that, remind me to spend more time with You, soaking in Your delight.

Held Steady

*"You'll be built solid, grounded in righteousness,
far from any trouble—nothing to fear!"*
<small>ISAIAH 54:14 MSG</small>

Belief in God's promises leads to a grace-filled life. One of the meanings of *grace* is "effortless beauty of movement." A person with this kind of grace doesn't trip over her own feet; she's not clumsy or awkward, but instead, she moves easily, fluidly, steadily. From a spiritual perspective, most of us stumble quite a bit. . .and yet we don't give up. We know that God holds our hands, and He will keep us steady, even when we would otherwise fall flat on our faces.

Balance isn't something we can achieve ourselves. Just when we think we have it all together, life has a tendency to come crashing down around our ears. But even in the midst of life's most chaotic moments, God keeps us balanced in His love. Like a building that's built to sway in an earthquake without falling down, as we believe in His promises, He will keep us grounded.

Lord of endless love, I believe You will keep me steady, even when my life seems to be falling apart at the seams. I trust in Your promises.

God's Ever-Present Love

*So I decided there is nothing better than to enjoy food
and drink and to find satisfaction in work. Then I realized
that these pleasures are from the hand of God.*
ECCLESIASTES 2:24 NLT

The author of Ecclesiastes had given up on finding any deeper, more eternal meaning in his life, so he decided to be a hedonist. Hedonists are people who believe life's only meaning lies in physical pleasures. But despite their belief, they can't escape God's love. Our food, our drink, the satisfaction we take in our work, our intimate relationships with our spouses, and all the physical pleasures of our lives are not separate from God. Instead, they are expressions of His love and blessing. It's a little like the old children's book *The Runaway Bunny*: no matter where the little bunny went, he found his mother already there; he discovered her love already embedded in each of his so-called escapes from her presence.

Bitterness and hurt can make us decide to turn away from belief in God—but no matter what we believe about Him, His love for us remains unchanged. As the psalmist discovered, "I can never escape from your Spirit! I can never get away from your presence!" (Psalm 139:7 NLT). But why would we want to?

*Spirit of love, I believe You will never leave me. Even if I
deny Your reality, Your loving presence is always with me.*

Resting in God

"Only in returning to me and resting in me will you be saved."
ISAIAH 30:15 NLT

We'd like to believe we can save ourselves from the messes we get ourselves into. We want to believe that we can rely on our own abilities and strengths, that we are competent and independent people. But sooner or later, that belief comes crashing down around our heads. Some days we try everything we can think of to save ourselves—but no matter how hard we try, we fail again and again. We fall on our faces and embarrass ourselves. We hurt the people around us. We make mistakes, and nothing whatsoever seems to go right.

When that happens, it's time to take a break and reconsider the faulty premise that's underlying our efforts. Belief in our abilities is healthy, but we also need to remember that our abilities and strengths are limited. Only God's love and creative power have no limits. Belief in His promises allows us to step back and stop trying so hard. Then we can rest in God's arms, knowing He will save us.

God, I believe Your love is my salvation. Remind me not to rely on my own efforts, when instead I need to rest in Your arms.

You're Never Alone!

O Lord, you know all about this. Do not stay silent.
Do not abandon me now, O Lord.
Psalm 35:22 nlt

Have you ever seen a child suddenly look up from playing, realize she's all alone, and then run to find her mother? Meanwhile, her mother was watching her all along. You may have had that experience with God: you looked around at your life and believed He had abandoned you, when all along His loving eye was on you.

Sometimes solitude is a good thing; but other times, it's just plain lonely. When loneliness turns into isolation, remember that God is always lovingly watching you. He sees what is happening in your life, and He will never abandon you to deal with it alone. Believe in His constant and watchful love—and you will experience the blessings He longs to give you.

I believe You are always with me, Lord, watching everything that happens in my life. Nothing is hidden from You, and Your love knows no limits.

Joyful Song

*The Lord is my strength and my shield; my heart trusts in him,
and he helps me. My heart leaps for joy, and with my song I praise him.*
PSALM 28:7 NIV

God proves Himself to us over and over again—and yet over and over, we doubt His power. We need to learn from experience. When doubts assail us, making it hard for us to believe in the promises God has given us, we need to look back at our lives and remind ourselves of what He has done for us in the past. The God whose love and strength rescued us yesterday and the day before will certainly rescue us again today. As we celebrate the blessings we received in the past, we gain confidence and faith for today and tomorrow. Our lives will be blessed with joy.

*You are my strength, Lord. I believe You will always be there to help
me and protect me. May my belief in You fill my life with joyful song.*

Wonderful Beyond Your Imagination

May he give you the desire of your heart and make all your plans succeed.
PSALM 20:4 NIV

There's a belief that's been going around for a while that has various names. Some people call it "the secret"; others refer to it as "the power of positive thinking" or "the law of attraction." There's even a Christian version that's sometimes known as "the prosperity gospel." This belief says that if we picture what we want in life, we will "attract" that thing; focusing on our hopes and wishes will turn them into a reality. And while there's some truth to the belief that focusing on the positive can shape our lives positively, there's no magic we can accomplish simply by the power of our thoughts. Just because we *want* something to happen doesn't mean it will, no matter how hard we pray or wish or hope. But when we truly commit everything we do to God, praying only for His love to be given free rein in our lives, then we may be surprised by what comes about. It may not be what we imagined—but it will be wonderful, and it will fulfill the deepest desires of our hearts.

Lord, I believe You want to give me the desires of my heart. I give You all my plans, all my hopes and wishes. I trust You to know more than I do about how my yearning heart will be most satisfied.

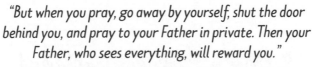

Private Prayer

"But when you pray, go away by yourself, shut the door behind you, and pray to your Father in private. Then your Father, who sees everything, will reward you."
MATTHEW 6:6 NLT

The world is full of a variety of beliefs about prayer. A 2017 Barna research study found that prayer is not only the most common faith practice among American adults, but it's also one of the most complex and multifaceted. The Bible speaks of numerous kinds of prayer (supplication, intercession, and worship, for example) and uses a range of ideas to describe the practice, telling us that prayer takes many shapes and forms. There's the corporate kind of prayer, where we lift our hearts to God as part of a congregation. There's also the far less elaborate kind of prayer that's said quickly and on the run—the whispered cry for help or a song of praise in the midst of life's busyness. But verses like this one tell us we need to make some time in our lives for the prayer that comes out of solitude—when, in the privacy of some quiet place, we come into God's presence all alone. Fortunately, the Barna study found that this is the form of prayer that 95 percent of Americans believe in most, with only 5 percent indicating they most believe in corporate prayer or prayer with at least one other person. God promises to bless this belief!

I believe, Lord, that prayer and solitude are necessary parts of my life. I believe You hear my prayers, and You will use prayer to bring Your love and blessing into my life.

Believe in Jesus' Teaching!

"Let me teach you, because I am humble and gentle at heart, and you will find rest for your souls."
MATTHEW 11:29 NLT

Sometimes we keep trying to do life on our own, even though we don't know what we're doing, even though we're exhausted. Somehow we believe we have to just keep stumbling on; we believe we have no other options. And all the while, Jesus waits quietly, ready to show us the way. He yearns to lead us with His quiet, gentle strength, carrying our burdens for us. We don't have to try so hard. We can let go of the belief that we have to do it on our own—and simply rest our souls in His presence.

Jesus, I believe You have everything I need in life—love, wisdom, strength, creativity. Thank You that You offer Yourself to me so humbly, so gently.

Believe in a God Who's Stronger Than Your Enemies!

My times are in your hands; deliver me from the hands of my enemies, from those who pursue me.
PSALM 31:15 NIV

Do you ever believe that trouble is chasing you? No matter how fast you run or how you try to hide, it comes after you relentlessly, dogging your footsteps, breathing its hot breath down your neck, robbing you of peace. What's even worse is that it doesn't only follow you; it waits for you down the road as well! Maybe you need to stop running and stop hiding and instead let yourself drop into God's hands, believing He will hold both the present and your future safe. No matter what form your "enemies" take, He is stronger than they are!

Faithful Lord, I believe You hold my life in Your hands. I don't need to worry about either present or future dangers, because You have everything under control. You will let no enemy—whether spiritual or physical—defeat me.

Believe in Your Inner Beauty!

*What matters is not your outer appearance—the styling of your hair,
the jewelry you wear, the cut of your clothes—but your inner disposition.
Cultivate inner beauty, the gentle, gracious kind that God delights in.*
1 Peter 3:3–4 msg

We want to be pretty. It's a longing that has been whispered into our hearts ever since we were little girls. Disney movies told us we had to look like a princess; Barbie dolls said we needed to be both skinny and curvy; and countless TV shows and commercials promised that pretty women are the ones who are most loved. As grown-up women, we often still believe that our appearance matters more than it does—that our hair, our clothes, our makeup are necessary ingredients to the persona we present to the world. Although God delights in our physical beings and wants us to care for and respect our bodies, we can become overly worried about our appearance, fretting over whether we measure up to the demanding standards of that little girl who still lives in our hearts. We need to replace that old childish belief in the necessity of princess-perfect prettiness with a new and stronger belief in our spiritual value. As we allow God's Spirit to shine through us, our deepest, truest beauty will be revealed.

*Spirit, I believe my true beauty comes from Your presence
in my heart. Shine through me so that others see You.*

Belief and the Imagination

*Now faith is confidence in what we hope for and assurance about
what we do not see. . . . Without faith it is impossible to please
God, because anyone who comes to him must believe that he
exists and that he rewards those who earnestly seek him.*

HEBREWS 11:1, 6 NIV

You believe in God, but sometimes your belief wavers. So how can
you bolster your belief in God? Try using the power of your imagination. Children are good at make-believe; but as adults, we've often
forgotten this mental skill. While it's true that our imaginations can
get us into trouble, an imagination that's guided by scripture and the
Spirit is a gift from God.

Try this: As you scrub the kitchen floor, imagine that Jesus will
walk across it. As you prepare a report at work, imagine that Jesus will
review it. As you do the family laundry, imagine that Jesus will wear
the clean clothes. Or as you go for a walk, picture Jesus walking beside
you, keeping you company. At night, when you can't sleep, pretend
you are being rocked in God's arms. This is no make-believe game.
Our imagination allows us to catch a glimpse of spiritual realities our
physical eyes are unable to see. It can strengthen our belief in God,
transforming an intellectual idea that lives only in our minds into an
emotional reality that gives shape and meaning to our everyday lives.

Use my imagination, Lord, to strengthen my belief in Your promises.

Daily Belief

In all your ways acknowledge Him, and He shall direct your paths.
PROVERBS 3:6 NKJV

Abraham Lincoln is believed to have said, "The best thing about the future is that it comes only one day at a time." God doesn't ask us to make a map of our entire life's journey. He simple asks us to give Him each day as it comes, morning by morning, night by night. Imagine if you had to determine right now how you would live each moment of the rest of your life. It would be an impossible task! Instead, relax in the belief that God will direct you *today*. Then make the same claim tomorrow, once again believing that as you commit the day to God, He will lead you. This practice of daily belief creates a lifetime of companionship with God.

Lord, I thank You that You never ask me to have my life all mapped out ahead of time. I believe in Your promise of guidance. I give You this day to use as You want. Remind me to do the same thing again tomorrow!

Believe in God's Grace!

For the grace of God has been revealed, bringing salvation to all people.
TITUS 2:11 NLT

The Greek word that's translated as "grace" is *charis*, a word connected to rejoicing that also implies sweetness, loveliness, favor, goodwill, and kindness. The word occurs in the New Testament at least 170 times! Our English versions have translated the same word in different ways, all of which help us get a fuller picture of what grace looks like. In some places, it has to do with gratitude and thanks. (This is why we "say grace" before a meal.) In other translations, it comes to us as "bounty," "liberality," or "generosity." Sometimes it seems like a joyful, sweet *feeling* we experience; sometimes it appears to be more like an *act* of mercy and love; other times, it appears to be a word that describes a *quality* of utter loveliness; and still others, it looks like something that is given, an undeserved *gift*.

The Greek word has one more shade of meaning that doesn't often come through in English: it has to do with God reaching toward us, a sense of God stretching across the distance between Himself and us, a divine act of leaning forward in eager love. Ultimately, grace takes many forms—but it is always something beautiful God holds out to us in His outstretched arms.

God, I believe in the power of Your grace to fill my heart and life.

Discipline and Learning

To learn, you must love discipline.
PROVERBS 12:1 NLT

Discipline. It's a word that has a range of beliefs attached to it, many of them negative. Sometimes it summons memories of disapproving grade-school teachers. But when the Bible talks about discipline, it isn't referring to scoldings and being sent to the principal's office. It's not talking about criticism and punishment. Instead, the Bible's discipline is always connected to learning. It has to do with developing the skills you need to live the full life God wants for you. The English word *discipline* also comes from similar root meanings: "instruction given, teaching, learning, knowledge." Think about what it takes to learn a sport or to play an instrument. It requires the willingness to hear and learn, the commitment to practice, and the patience to keep going despite stumbles and setbacks. That's discipline! In the Bible, discipline is a good thing—something that makes you stronger, more skillful, more capable. So erase any leftover negative beliefs from childhood you have about discipline—and replace them with the joy and excitement that comes from learning and growing with God.

*Heavenly Teacher, I believe I have so much to learn
from You. May I be Your willing and disciplined student.*

The Empowerment of Blessing

God can pour on the blessings in astonishing ways so that you're ready for anything and everything, more than just ready to do what needs to be done.
2 CORINTHIANS 9:8 MSG

Blessings are God's love to you in tangible form. Sometimes they are so small you nearly overlook them—the sun on your face, the smile of a friend, or food on the table—but other times they are so great that you are overcome with amazement. Day by day, God's blessing makes you ready for whatever comes your way. As you believe in His promises, He gives you exactly what you need. He empowers you for each challenge you face so that His blessings can pass through you to others, spreading His love to each person you encounter.

God, I believe You love me endlessly—and this means You are constantly blessing me. Remind me not to ignore the expressions of Your love that are everywhere I turn. Keep me sensitive to what You are doing in my life so that Your Spirit will fill me with the strength and love I need to serve You.

Believe in the World's Ultimate Freedom!

Creation waits in eager expectation for the children of God to be revealed. For the creation was subjected. . .in hope that the creation itself will be liberated from its bondage to decay and brought into the freedom and glory of the children of God.
ROMANS 8:19–21 NIV

Some days, it's hard to feel very optimistic. As we listen to the evening news and hear story after story about natural disasters and human greed, it's difficult to believe God has a triumphant and joyful plan in store for our world. Instead, it looks more like everything is falling apart! God doesn't want us to be ostriches, hiding our heads in the sand, refusing to acknowledge what's going on in the world; there is real suffering and injustice out there, and we should not shut our eyes or pretend it doesn't matter. But God also wants us to believe that the future is full of wonderful things He has planned. All creation is holding its breath, waiting for God's wonderful love to fully reveal itself and set both the natural world and the human world free from their bondage to brokenness and pain.

Creator, I believe You have amazing, beautiful things in store for the world You made. Despite the violence, prejudice, suffering, and conflict that are so common, Your love is constantly at work. Use me to further Your work of love on this earth.

Success

*"You will succeed in whatever you choose to do,
and light will shine on the road ahead of you."*
JOB 22:28 NLT

A recent sociological study found that men and women tend to have different beliefs about success. Women in the study highlighted the importance of a balance between work and relationships, whereas men focused more on material success. Both sexes, however, believed that success is something that has both external manifestations and internal, emotional rewards. However people define it, everyone longs to be successful!

The word *success* originally meant simply "the thing that comes next." Over the years, we've added to that meaning the sense that success has to be the thing we *wanted* to happen, the outcome we hoped for. But God does not necessarily define success the way we do. Whatever comes next, no matter what, His love transforms it, using circumstances to shape us into the complete and joyful people He created us to be. So if you've been feeling disappointed in your life or yourself, take a look at your beliefs about success. Do they line up with God's definition?

*God, I believe You can use even the things I perceive as failures
as openings for Your creative love to flow out into the world.*

Believe in Your Gifts!

God's various gifts are handed out everywhere; but they all originate in God's Spirit. God's various ministries are carried out everywhere; but they all originate in God's Spirit. God's various expressions of power are in action everywhere; but God himself is behind it all. Each person is given something to do that shows who God is: Everyone gets in on it, everyone benefits. All kinds of things are handed out by the Spirit, and to all kinds of people! The variety is wonderful.

1 Corinthians 12:4–8 msg

Do you ever look around at other people's gifts and talents and believe you don't measure up by comparison? This belief can interfere with what God wants to do through you. God shines through each of us in different ways. One person is good at expressing herself in words; another is good with children; and still another has a gift for giving wise advice to her friends. Whatever our gifts are, they all come from God. They are all tangible expressions of His love, and each one reveals God's Spirit to the world.

Holy Spirit, I believe You have gifted me with abilities that demonstrate God's reality. Let no self-doubt or false modesty interfere with me using these gifts to spread Your love.

Believe in Your Creativity!

"[God's] filled him with the Spirit of God, with skill, ability, and know-how for making all sorts of things, to design and work in gold, silver, and bronze; to carve stones and set them; to carve wood, working in every kind of skilled craft. . . . He's gifted them with the know-how needed for carving, designing, weaving, and embroidering in blue, purple, and scarlet fabrics, and in fine linen. They can make anything and design anything."
EXODUS 35:31–33, 35 MSG

God made human beings in His own image—and that included the ability to be creative. Whether we sew clothes or paint pictures, come up with new business ideas or write stories, make a welcoming home or cook delicious meals, God's creativity longs to be expressed through us. As we believe in our own unique creative talents and put them to use, we are united with God's Spirit. He works through our hands, using us to add to creation as we make the world a lovelier place for us all.

Spirit, once again I affirm my belief in the gifts You have given me, including the ability to be creative. Remove any self-doubt that blocks my creativity. May I take delight in being creative, allowing Your inspiration to use my talents.

Time

Your throne, O LORD, has stood from time immemorial.
You yourself are from the everlasting past.
PSALM 93:2 NLT

Time is a mysterious thing even scientists don't understand. Albert Einstein proposed that time is an illusion, something that depends on human perception. Einstein also came up with the idea that time could be a fourth dimension, as well as the idea that time might move differently depending on our circumstances. Some scientists speculate that time could behave differently in different parts of the cosmos. For most of us, though, time is such a constant part of our lives that we assume we understand how it works. We usually believe it is like a fast-moving river we are caught in, a stream that constantly carries us into the future while the past rushes away behind us. Life keeps slipping away from us like water between our fingers.

But the Bible tells us that time will not exist forever; someday it will come to an end (Revelation 10:6). God is outside time's stream. He holds our past safe in His hands, and His love is permanent and unshakable. Our belief in Him is the lifesaver we cling to in the midst of time's wild waves.

Lord, I believe You are greater than time itself.
You hold past, present, and future in Your hands.

A Lot or a Little

I'm just as happy with little as with much, with much as with little.
I've found the recipe for being happy whether full or hungry, hands
full or hands empty. Whatever I have, wherever I am, I can make
it through anything in the One who makes me who I am.
PHILIPPIANS 4:12–13 MSG

When you were younger, what did you believe you needed to be happy? Nice clothes? A good job? Lots of friends? And now? What do you believe your happiness requires? Your beliefs can either limit or expand the happiness you actually experience. Day after day, God blesses you—but your happiness does not depend on those blessings. Your joy and contentment depend only on God. When that belief sinks in deep, you no longer have to worry about losing or gaining life's blessings.

Giver of life, I believe that whether I have little or a lot,
I will always have enough. Thank You for Your constant
blessing. Thank You for making me who I am.

Don't Believe in Idols!

"Stay away from idols! I am the one who answers your prayers and cares for you. I am like a tree that is always green; all your fruit comes from me."
HOSEA 14:8 NLT

Of course I don't believe in idols, you may say to yourself as you read this verse. You don't pray to a wooden statue or bow down and worship a creature carved from stone. But when the Bible talks about idols, it's referring to anything that takes God's rightful place in your life. The Hebrew word used in this verse refers to something that's been fabricated (something that doesn't occur naturally), but it also has to do with something that ultimately causes pain and suffering. This is the exact opposite of the true God's nature. God always listens and cares. He is like a tree growing at the center of your life, constantly offering you shelter and nourishment. Each one of life's daily blessings is a fruit from this tree; each time you grow and learn, that too is divine fruit ripening in your life.

Tree of Life, I believe only You can satisfy my longings for growth, refreshment, shelter, and nourishment. Show me if I have allowed any idols to encroach on Your place in my life.

150

Companionship in Suffering

Singing cheerful songs to a person with a heavy heart is like taking someone's coat in cold weather or pouring vinegar in a wound.
PROVERBS 25:20 NLT

We live in a culture that believes we really *ought* to be happy all the time—and if we're not, there's something wrong. This can make it hard for us to interact with those who are suffering. Perhaps you've noticed how uncomfortable it feels to be with someone who just lost her job or is going through a painful divorce. You want to help change her mood. . .but in doing so, you may be denying her right to her painful feelings. Rather than trying to cheer her up, often the most helpful thing you can do is empathize. Listen. Affirm her pain. Verify her disappointment. Your understanding allows her to accept herself so she can eventually move on, in her own time. God ultimately will use this time in her life to bless her. In the meantime, it's not your job to "fix" her or her life. Your job is to simply be her companion through the pain, allowing God's love to use you in whatever way He sees fit.

God, when my friends are in pain, I believe only You can heal their hearts. May I be a good friend who is willing to listen, a faithful companion who will share their suffering.

You Are Never Forgotten!

But Zion said, "The LORD has forsaken me, the Lord has forgotten me."
ISAIAH 49:14 NIV

Sometimes God allows a long period of pain and hardship in our lives. When that happens, we often start to doubt the promises we once believed. We think God has given up on us. Or maybe we believe that God doesn't actually care about us—or that He doesn't even exist. With our human limitations, we find ways like these to explain to ourselves why God hasn't rescued us from the trouble we're experiencing. If we don't sense He is present with us and we don't see Him saving us from our dilemma, we assume He has forgotten us and given up on us.

But look at what God says in reply when we feel this way: "Can a mother forget the baby at her breast and have no compassion on the child she has borne? Though she may forget, I will not forget you!" (Isaiah 49:15 NIV). What a strong picture of God's love! Then in the next verse, He emphasizes His love even further: "See, I have written your name on My hand" (see Isaiah 49:16).

God will never forget you. He will never give up on you. He will never stop loving you.

Thank You, Lord, that Your love for me is even greater than a mother's for her baby. Despite the difficult circumstances of my life, I believe You will never stop loving me.

Believe in Equality!

The rich and the poor shake hands as equals—GOD made them both!
PROVERBS 22:2 MSG

Americans often affirm their belief in the equality of all people—but at the same time, not all Americans have the same access to privileges and opportunities. This reality rises to the surface again and again throughout our nation's history. Sometimes, we try to push it down, out of sight. We'd much rather believe that the American dream is possible for everyone; it's painful to face the fact that some people experience danger, hardship, and unequal opportunities, simply because of the color of their skin or some other difference that sets them apart from "the rest of us."

Long before today's struggle for social justice, the Bible reminded human beings that God is the Creator of us all—whether we are rich, poor, dark, light, quick, or slow. We all have the right to breathe, think, act, speak, and live freely.

Lord of justice, I believe You created us all to be equals. Make me aware of any prejudice within me that interferes with Your all-inclusive love. Use me as a force for justice in my community.

Love Made Visible

*No one has ever seen God. But if we love each other, God lives
in us, and his love is brought to full expression in us.*
1 John 4:12 nlt

It's hard to believe in something we can't see. As human beings, most of us (those of us who have vision) depend on our eyes to understand the world around us. We've all heard the saying "A picture is worth a thousand words," and the advertising world knows the power of visual images to influence our minds. So do teachers. Abstract concepts are difficult to wrap our minds around—but if we can see something, it instantly becomes easier for us to grasp.

As John points out, none of us have seen God. We know we are told to walk by faith rather than sight (see 2 Corinthians 5:7)—and yet all of us, at one time or another, have had a hard time believing in God's love. In a world where terrible things happen, we can't help but wonder if God's love is real. Is *God* even real? It's hard to believe in something we've never seen. We need a visual image to convince us.

Jesus was that visual image. And now, as His followers, we are called to carry out His work on earth. He wants us each to be a visible embodiment of God's love. Through us, love becomes visible. We are the expression of God to the world.

*Jesus, I believe You are the embodiment of God's love.
May I too carry divine love out into the world.*

Belief in God's Love

"This is how much God loved the world: He gave his Son, his one and only Son. And this is why: so that no one need be destroyed; by believing in him, anyone can have a whole and lasting life. God didn't go to all the trouble of sending his Son merely to point an accusing finger, telling the world how bad it was. He came to help, to put the world right again."
JOHN 3:16–17 MSG

There are different kinds of belief. For example, we believe the sun will rise in the morning; we expect it to happen, because it has always happened. We no longer believe in Santa Claus, as we may have once done when we were children; we acknowledge that Santa is probably not a real person. Meanwhile, we may believe in God as an intellectual concept, something distant and almost irrelevant that we take for granted. But the word that's used in John 3:16 is a different sort of belief. The Greek word implies an active involvement, rather than a mere matter of the mind. It speaks to the idea that we need to commit our entire life to belief; we entrust ourselves to God, and in doing so, we participate in making our belief stronger. The Greek word also indicates that God is part of this process. He works within us to increase our belief in Him. According to *Thayer's Greek Lexicon*, the word *belief* as it's used in these verses from the Gospel of John "signif[ies] that one's faith is preserved, strengthened, increased, raised to the level which it ought to reach."

Jesus, I believe You came to bring me the fullness of life, the complete potential for which I was created. Thank You that You are always working in me to increase my belief in You.

155

Blessing Instead of Cursing

"Bless those who curse you. Pray for those who hurt you."
Luke 6:28 NLT

When we believe in God's promise, He blesses us; but we are also called to bless others. God wants to show the world His love through us. We accomplish this through prayer—and through our commitment to make God's love real in the world around us. We offer blessings to others when we greet a scowl with a smile, when we refuse to respond to angry words, and when we offer understanding to those who are angry and hurt. Belief in God is never meant to be a private, personal thing. It is always intended to spread out from us, touching everyone we interact with.

Lord of love, I believe You have called me to be Your coworker, sharing in Your work of spreading love to all people. Help me bless instead of curse; may I make a practice of offering loving prayer for those who have hurt me. Please use me in whatever way You can to show Your love.

Celebrate!

Seize life! Eat bread with gusto, drink wine with a robust heart.
Oh yes—God takes pleasure in your pleasure! Dress festively every morning.
Don't skimp on colors and scarves. Relish life with the spouse you love
each and every day of your precarious life. Each day is God's gift.
ECCLESIASTES 9:7–9 MSG

These verses may not seem consistent with the God many of us were raised to believe in. But the truth is God longs to make us happy. He knows that happiness is good for us. Mentally and physically, we function better when we are happy. Discouragement and sadness sap our strength. It's like trying to work while carrying a heavy load on our backs: it slows us down and makes everything harder.

Believe that God wants you to be strong and happy! He doesn't want you to creep through life with a pinched look of disapproval and displeasure on your face. No. He wants you to celebrate! He wants everyone to see the joy you feel as you receive His daily blessings.

God of joy, I believe You take pleasure in my pleasure. Give me a
joyful heart. Remind me to rejoice in the life You've given me. Make
my happiness contagious so that those around me catch Your joy.

This World Is Not Your Home

"Everything comes from you; all we're doing is giving back what we've been given from your generous hand. As far as you're concerned, we're homeless, shiftless wanderers like our ancestors, our lives mere shadows. . . . I know, dear God, that you care nothing for the surface—you want us, our true selves."
1 Chronicles 29:14–15, 17 msg

We look at the world around us, and part of us believes it's the only home we'll ever know. We've never experienced any other reality, and we can't imagine the far greater world God inhabits. But we are not meant to feel too at home in this world. Maybe that's why time is designed to keep us from lingering too long in one place; it keeps taking away the things we depended on, pushing us constantly into new experiences. Each new relationship, each new circumstance, each new role in life—all come from the God who sees the eternal meaning that lies beneath the surface of our lives. We are not meant to cling too tightly to anything in this life. Instead, God calls us to be always moving on, making our way to our forever home in heaven.

Heavenly Father, I believe all my "possessions" are expressions of Your love. Remind me to let go of them when the time comes, filled with the joyful anticipation of what You'll do next in my life.

Earthly Tents

For we know that when this earthly tent we live in is taken down (that is, when we die and leave this earthly body), we will have a house in heaven, an eternal body made for us by God himself and not by human hands.

2 CORINTHIANS 5:1 NLT

Scripture says that God has "set eternity in the human heart" (Ecclesiastes 3:11 NIV). We have a sense that life goes on beyond what exists on this earth—and yet we cannot see what lies beyond death's door. So we tend to hold on tightly to this life, believing that since this is all we know, this must be all there is. The writers of the New Testament often remind us, however, that life is temporary. In this verse, Paul compares our bodies to tents: dwelling places that are not intended to be permanent. A tent is a useful thing to have on a journey; it can provide shelter, keeping out the wind and rain. But few people would want to settle down and live in a tent for the rest of their lives. If we can hold on to the thought that our bodies are like tents, intended only to be temporary shelters during this life's journey, perhaps we'll find it easier to believe in the eternal bodies God will give us.

God, I believe my life will not end when my body dies. When the time comes for me to take down the "tent" that has sheltered me through this life, may I be ready for the new life You have ready for me.

Everything Is Under Control

Trust GOD from the bottom of your heart;
don't try to figure out everything on your own.
PROVERBS 3:5 MSG

Doubts come. They're part of your inherent humanness. God knows that. Things have happened to you that make trusting Him seem foolish. It can feel like the ultimate paradox to release the self-protections you've worked so hard to cultivate. Yet God loves you and wants to ease your fear and anxiety. Picture this: unclenching the fist of your heart and releasing the problems you've tried relentlessly to figure out on your own, placing them each into God's outstretched hands. You don't have to go through life alone, always on guard. God waits patiently for you to believe He has everything under control.

God, I believe You are completely, totally, utterly trustworthy.
I know You hold my life in Your hands—and You will never let it drop.

Intentional Love

Love never gives up.
1 CORINTHIANS 13:4 MSG

Love may be a spiritual quality, but it's also as down to earth and as practical as the air we breathe. As human beings, we need love. In fact, psychologists tell us that love is as necessary to our lives as oxygen. The more connected we are to others and to God, the healthier we will be—both physically and emotionally—and the less connected we are, the more we are at risk.

Our culture tends to believe that love "just happens." If we don't feel enough love in our lives, then we're just not one of the lucky people. If we find it hard to love someone, oh well—that's just the way it is. But love doesn't work that way. Psychologist Erich Fromm called love "an act of will." To feel love in our lives, we have to make up our minds to act in loving ways. We have to put our love for God and others into practice.

Jesus, I believe You call me to practice Your selfless love in all my interactions. Teach me to follow in Your footsteps, no matter how unloving I may feel.

The Riches of Belief

Whoever trusts in the LORD will be enriched.
PROVERBS 28:25 NRSV

We speak of faith in a variety of ways. Is it the church we attend? The creed we follow? Those things may be expressions of our faith, and they may help to support and nurture our faith, but the faith the Bible talks about is deeper than that. It involves confidence in God's ability to finish what He started in us, trusting He will do what we can't figure out for ourselves. Personal faith means loosening our grip on our family, job, circumstances, and future. Belief in God's infinite strength and love allows us to let go—not because we no longer care about those things, but because we are confident God's love is big enough to hold each one of them. In this letting go, we find freedom and life. We are made rich with the peace and joy of Jesus.

I believe in You, Jesus. I believe I can trust my life to Your love.
Thank You for all the ways I am enriched by my belief.

The Lord Is Your Hope and Confidence

"But blessed are those who trust in the LORD and have made the LORD their hope and confidence."
JEREMIAH 17:7 NLT

What gives you confidence? Is it your clothes, your money, your skills? These are all good things, but they are blessings from God, given to you from His grace. When your hopes (in other words, your expectations for the future) rest only in God, then you can head out confidently into each new day, knowing He will never disappoint you.

Lord, I believe that everything in my life comes from You. Teach me to put my confidence in You, rather than in any ability of my own. I believe You are the fulfillment of all my hopes.

Healthy and Strong

*My health may fail, and my spirit may grow weak, but God
remains the strength of my heart; he is mine forever.*
PSALM 73:26 NLT

Sooner or later, our bodies let us down. Even the healthiest of us will one day have to face old age. When our bodies' strength fails us, we may feel discouraged and depressed. We may even find ourselves doubting God's love and care for us. With renewed faith, however, we can find joy and strength in our God. When our hearts belong to the Creator of the universe, we realize we are far more than our bodies. Because of God's unfailing love, we will be truly healthy for all eternity.

*Creator, I believe that no matter what happens to my body,
You never stop blessing me. When sickness strikes me and as
I age, remind me that You continue to make me strong.*

With All Your Heart

*Trust in the LORD with all your heart
and lean not on your own understanding.*
PROVERBS 3:5 NIV

Life is confusing. No matter how hard we try, we can't always make sense of it. We don't like it when that happens, and so we keep trying to determine what's going on—as though we were trying puzzle piece after puzzle piece to fill in a picture we long to see. Sometimes, though, we have to accept that in this life we'll never be able to see the entire image. We have to believe that God holds the missing pieces we can't yet see.

Lord, I believe You always see the big picture; You understand all that my mind still can't grasp. Help me trust You with all my heart—my total inner being—relying on You rather than my own sense of how things work.

"Normal" Life

Dear friends, don't be surprised at the fiery trials you are going through, as if something strange were happening to you. Instead, be very glad—for these trials make you partners with Christ in his suffering, so that you will have the wonderful joy of seeing his glory when it is revealed to all the world.

1 PETER 4:12–13 NLT

Most of us tend to believe that troubles and trials are something out of the ordinary; when they come, we long for life to get back to "normal." We believe life *should* go along smoothly. Sometimes, of course, it does—at least for a while. Sooner or later (and often sooner rather than later), problems come along: an illness, a financial need, a criticism that wounds our hearts, a disagreement with a loved one. Whatever it is, we're surprised each time, outraged even. "This isn't the way life is *supposed* to be!" we insist.

In these verses, however, Peter tells us that trials and troubles *are* normal. They're just a part of life. But being "very glad" in the middle of trials seems to be going way too far! Notice, though, that Peter doesn't say we're to be glad *because of* our trials. No, we're to be glad because we believe God's promise of the comfort, growth, and deeper intimacy with Him that He will bring to us through all of life's tribulations.

Loving God, I believe You will use even the problems and crises I encounter in life to bless me in ways I can't imagine. I trust You to be with me no matter what trials I face.

Preparing for the Future

*Don't for a minute envy careless rebels; soak yourself
in the Fear-of-God—that's where your future lies.
Then you won't be left with an armload of nothing.*
PROVERBS 23:17–18 MSG

We'd like to believe we can plan ahead for life's dangers. Certainly, there are things we can do that will help us be better prepared: taking care of our bodies now will help us have a healthier old age; saving for retirement can ensure that our needs are met when we no longer have income from our jobs; life insurance can provide for our family's needs if we were to die suddenly. It's wise to take these precautions—but no one can predict exactly what the future holds.

Sometimes, it may seem as though others around us have better luck than we do; it may even seem that people who cheated or were unkind to others ended up ahead of us. These verses in Proverbs, however, tell us not to compare ourselves to others. Instead, they remind us that our future security depends on our relationship with God now. If we rely on anything else, we'll end up with empty hands and empty hearts.

*Lord, I believe You have a plan for my future, a plan
that will carry me through old age and all the way into
eternity with You. I'm relying on You to keep me safe.*

Believe God Wants You to Be Happy!

This is the day which the LORD hath made; we will rejoice and be glad in it.
PSALM 118:24 KJV

Sometimes, we believe that taking time for pleasure, laughter, and play is irresponsible. Our culture insists we have to be *productive* in some way, every minute we're awake. With so much we're responsible for, so much we have to accomplish every day, we don't have time for the sort of joy that children take for granted. The days just aren't long enough, we tell ourselves. No matter how much we rush, no matter how busy we are, no matter how frantically we hurry from one task to another, we can never get caught up. And meanwhile, the years keep going by, and we keep getting older and older. The minutes of our lives are like coins that slip away from our grasp all too quickly.

Imagine a child throwing coins into a fountain; she doesn't care if she's wasting money. She only knows she's having fun—and by having fun, she spreads her joy to everyone who sees her. We can be the same with life's pleasures. Time is one of God's gifts to us, and we don't need to be afraid to "waste" it. Instead, we can make room in our lives for delight.

I believe, Lord, that You want me to take time to be happy. Today, surprise me with unexpected delights. Keep my eyes open and my mind alert so that I won't miss any of the pleasure You have in store for me.

Cooling Tension

*A quietly given gift soothes an irritable person;
a heartfelt present cools a hot temper.*
PROVERBS 21:14 MSG

When someone is cross with us, we believe we're justified in being cross too. It's just a knee-jerk reaction to snap back if a spouse or friend says something unkind. If a colleague shoots an angry remark in our direction, we assume we have the right to retaliate. The Bible suggests a different way of handling tension, though. When we offer the gift of a quiet response or an understanding word, our generous act can defuse the tension. Sometimes, a more tangible gift can also make a positive difference. It doesn't have to be elaborate or expensive. Homemade cookies, a lunch out, or an offer of help with a difficult project could be what it takes to cool a heated situation.

Jesus, You removed the old law that said an eye for an eye and a tooth for a tooth. Now I believe You want me to live in peace with the people in my life—and I believe Your example shows me the way to do that. Teach me to always speak and act with love as my goal.

A Child's Wisdom

"The greatest among you must become like the youngest."
LUKE 22:26 NRSV

As adults, we often believe we know more than the children in our lives. After all, we have far more experience and education. And while it's true that children depend on us for care and guidance, we may need to shift our beliefs a little when it comes to the children in our lives. In many ways, children are wiser than we are. We get so used to functioning in the adult world, loaded down with responsibilities, that we forget the child's knack for living in the present moment, for taking delight in small things, for loving unconditionally. Jesus asks us to let go of our grown-up dignity and allow ourselves to enter His presence as children. As we stop believing in our own importance and expertise, we will experience more deeply the blessings He is longing to give to us.

Jesus, I believe that if I want to follow You more closely, I need to have a child's heart. Take away my grown-up pride and arrogance. Give me the humility and simplicity I need to be more like You.

Holistic Health

He makes the whole body fit together perfectly. As each part does its own special work, it helps the other parts grow, so that the whole body is healthy and growing and full of love.
EPHESIANS 4:16 NLT

Western medicine has become more and more specialized. Although going to a medical specialist can have benefits, the belief that we are a collection of separate organs can also lead to treatment problems. The cardiologist may overlook the aspects of our diet and lifestyle that are contributing to heart disease; the dermatologist may not realize that our skin rash is caused by an ailing liver. God, on the other hand, has a holistic perspective on health. He doesn't see us as a collection of pieces, but as unified beings He longs to heal completely. He looks at our world in the same way, working to redeem the entire package: the environment, politics, education, health care, and everything else. Health pours out of Him, a daily stream of blessing we can rely on for each aspect of life.

Sometimes, Jesus, I believe what I do on Friday night won't hurt my relationship with You on Sunday morning. I believe I can harbor intolerance and impatience in my heart when I'm at work without it impacting our intimacy when I come to You in prayer that night. Convince me, I pray, that life is an interactive whole, each part contributing to the other.

Your Mind's Radio Station

Tune your ears to the world of Wisdom;
set your heart on a life of Understanding.
PROVERBS 2:2 MSG

Despite your best intentions, your beliefs will be shaped by the messages you absorb from the world around you. What voices do you listen to most? Do you pay attention to the messages that tell you to buy, buy, buy, to dress and look a certain way, to focus on things that won't last? Or have you tuned your ears to hear the quiet voice of God's wisdom? You can tell the answer to that question by your response to another question: What is most important to you? Things? Or the intangible blessing of true understanding? Your mind is a little like a radio station: you can choose which "station" you want to be tuned into. The more you tune into divine wisdom, the more steady will be your belief in God and His promises.

God of wisdom, I want to tune my spiritual reception to Your
frequency. I believe You are the source of all life and joy.

Sunshine

"[He] is like the light of morning when the sun comes up, a morning in which there are no clouds. He is like the brightness after rain that produces grass from the earth."
2 Samuel 23:4 net

Sometimes we start to believe our lives are nothing but gray days. From small frustrations to major crises, life can be so *hard.* With all our many responsibilities and troubles, we may even believe we'd be immature and shallow to dream of sunny days. Sunshine is for kids, we think; grown-up life is *serious.*

God is with us in our shadows of course—but He also made the sunshine, and He wants to share it with us. He wants us to believe that even the dreariest, darkest winters always give way to spring. And when the sun comes out, He doesn't want us to miss it! He calls us to come outside, to play, to laugh, to have a child's heart again.

So don't sit inside your dark house with the windows shut, brooding over life's troubles. And don't be so busy with your grown-up, indoor life that you miss the joy of light and fresh air. God has things He longs to share with you in the sunshine. He wants you to know the reality of His joy and taste the delight of His presence. He wants to see you smile, laugh—even play!

God of sunshine, I believe Your light is always shining, even when I can't see it. Keep me confident that no matter how dark the storm, sunny days lie ahead.

Enough

*Honor the LORD with your wealth and with
the best part of everything you produce.*
PROVERBS 3:9 NLT

Today, we believe the word *wealth* pertains mostly to money, but long ago, the word meant "happiness, prosperity, well-being." We also believe *wealth* has to do with having an excess of something—or having more of something than everyone else has. The Hebrew word used here in Proverbs, however, means sufficiency. It implies having enough, all that you need, rather than an excess. As we begin to reshape our beliefs about wealth, we can enter into the reality God wants us to inhabit. Instead of believing that we must earn more and more money, we realize wealth encompasses far more of our life than our finances. Our health, our abilities, our friends, our family, our physical strength, our creative energy—all of these are parts of our true wealth. God has given us exactly what we need of each one of these things; we have enough. With that belief firmly placed in our hearts and minds, we can then use this wealth to honor God.

*Generous Lord, I believe You have given me all that I need. In You,
I am truly wealthy. May I use all You have given me to honor You.*

The Natural World

"Walk out into the fields and look at the wildflowers."
MATTHEW 6:28 MSG

God's blessings are as near as the sky over your head or the grass beneath your feet. Look up—and be reminded of how wonderful God truly is. The same God who created the sun and the atmosphere, the stars and the galaxies, who day by day creates a new sunrise and a new sunset, that same God loves you and creates beauty in your life each day. Look down—and realize the incredible mystery of soil and roots that give nourishment to all life on planet Earth. Take the time to go outdoors. Look at nature. You don't have to spend hours outside to realize how beautifully God made the world. A single flower, if you really look at it, could be enough to fill you with awe. Sometimes, you only need something very simple to renew your belief in God's love and blessing.

Lord of life, I believe the natural world is full of Your beauty,
Your mystery, Your fertile creativity. Thank You for making
this lovely earth. May I honor it by honoring You, and may
the beauty around me lead me closer to Your heart.

Goodness

Walk in the way of goodness.
PROVERBS 2:20 NKJV

What do you believe about goodness? It's one of those words we use and assume we know what we mean, but it's actually rather hard to define. During the Victorian Age, *goodness* came to be equated with morality—following society's rules, especially those pertaining to sexuality. The older meaning of *goodness*, coming from the Middle Ages and earlier, had to do with unity and wholeness. According to the *New American Standard Concordance*, the Hebrew word used here in this verse from Proverbs contains these meanings (and more): beautiful, beneficial, cheerful, delightful, festive, generous, glad, gracious, happy, sweet, pleasing, ripe, completion, and soundness.

Archbishop Desmond Tutu, a Nobel Peace Prize recipient from South Africa, said, "The world is hungry for goodness." With so much hatred, power mongering, and intolerance in the world, people long for God's beautiful, delightful, generous, sweet, and fulfilling goodness. Our hearts yearn for goodness—*real* goodness, not just legalistic morality—and we long for the paths that will lead us to our hearts' desire.

Lord, I believe You are the source of all goodness—all sweetness, all joy, all beauty, and all fulfillment. Show me the path that leads to You, I pray, so that I may experience all the glad, generous, delightful goodness You have to offer.

Tough Times

God is good, a hiding place in tough times. He recognizes and welcomes anyone looking for help, no matter how desperate the trouble.
NAHUM 1:7 MSG

Do you ever feel as though you're stumbling around in the dark? If you're like many people, you may believe things aren't right if you can't see where you're going; most of us believe we *deserve* to see the road ahead. But it doesn't take faith to walk confidently in the bright sunlight of noon. Times like that, we can rely on our own intelligence and abilities. Faith comes into play during tough and desperate times, when we walk forward through pitch darkness, relying totally on the grasp of God's hand on ours for guidance. No trouble is too big for God!

I believe, God, that You are both my hiding place and my guide. You are my refuge from life's tough times—and You know the way that will lead me out of the darkness and into the light.

Gifts from the Lord

Ears to hear and eyes to see—both are gifts from the LORD.
PROVERBS 20:12 NLT

Everything you have is a gift from God. The air you breathe, the sunset that thrills you with its colors, the rain that nourishes your garden, the work that brings you satisfaction, the love of your family and friends, your taste buds, your physical strength, the music playing on the radio, a bird's song, the creativity you and others use to bring new things into the world—all these come from God and are proof of His love. As you believe in Him, you will find that your life brims over with blessing.

I believe, Lord, that You have given me all the things in life that give me joy and pleasure. You have filled my life with so many delights, so many treasures. May I never take them for granted.

Gladness

*Worship the L*ORD *with gladness. Come before him, singing with joy.*
PSALM 100:2 NLT

When did so many of us start believing that religion was a serious, somber affair? The Bible is full of happy words like *gladness*, *pleasure*, *song*, *praise*, *joy*, and *rejoice*. Nowhere does it say we should frown, sigh, disapprove, worry, be sad, criticize, or think about nothing but sin and sadness and death. That is definitely not what scripture says! And yet that's how we often act. We don't take seriously scripture's commandments to be joyful.

The Bible's joy is always connected to the presence of God. It is the natural state we find ourselves in if we walk with Him. It is the organic by-product of believing in God and His promises. Of course that doesn't mean we'll never be sad; but have you ever heard the saying "You may not be able to keep birds from perching on your head—but you can keep them from building nests in your hair"? It means we can't always control our emotions, but we *can* choose which ones we want to hold on to and dwell on.

*Lord of gladness, I believe Your love will daily bring me
joy—even in the midst of trouble and heartache. I trust
that Your joyful, loving presence is at work in my life.*

Bursting Barns

*Honor GOD with everything you own; give him
the first and the best. Your barns will burst.*
PROVERBS 3:9–10 MSG

Forget about the belief that you need to overwork, overdo, and keep it up 24-7 in order to please God. That belief comes from our culture's values, not from scripture, and all too often your inner bully will use that belief to clobber you with guilt and a sense of unworthiness. Silence the inner tyrant by naming what you're thankful for. Gratitude changes your focus. It's a way to honor God through the things He has given you. Sharing your blessings is another way to honor God. In return, He promises that your "barn"—the storehouse where you keep your treasures—will be so full that its walls will burst!

*God, I believe You have given me everything I need. Rather than
pushing myself harder and harder, now I can begin to rest in You.
May I always honor You through the things You have given me.*

Stop Believing You Know It All!

Don't be impressed with your own wisdom. Instead, fear the Lord and turn away from evil. Then you will have healing for your body and strength for your bones.

Proverbs 3:7–8 nlt

The Bible often speaks of "the fear of the Lord," but God doesn't want us to be afraid of Him. Instead, according to the *New American Standard Concordance*, "fear of the Lord" is about feeling awe and reverence when we come into God's presence. It has to do with setting aside our beliefs in our own wisdom, sufficiency, and independence so that we can acknowledge God's immense, unfathomable love and goodness. The concordance also says that the word *evil* in this verse refers to "calamity, adversity, harm, and hurt." In other words, when we stop believing that we know what's best for our lives—when we let go of our need to be know-it-alls—then we discover a new life of health, strength, and wholeness, a life that's free from the harm and damage that comes from sin. God's way always leads to our greatest well-being.

Lord of health and healing, I believe You always know what is best for me. When I doubt Your ways, remind me that Your love is always seeking to save me, heal me, and give me joy.

Worship

"God is spirit, and the people who worship him must worship in spirit and truth."
JOHN 4:24 NET

The word *worship* is one we may connect to singing praise songs or lifting our hearts in silent adoration to God. Those activities are aspects of worship, but the oldest roots of the word *worship* offer us a new perspective. "Worth-ship," the original English word used a thousand-some years ago, was based on a two-way relationship between a lord and his servant. The servant's "worth-ship" of the lord gave worth—valor, strength, and value—to the servant as well as the lord, for the two were linked together in a mutual commitment of honor and esteem.

Worship from this perspective is simply the daily practice of living out our belief in God. It involves a mutual commitment between God's Spirit and ours. We can express that commitment in all sorts of ways—from praise choruses to vocal prayer to total silence—but ultimately, it is the relationship itself that creates this two-way stream of love and honor. When we enter into this relationship with the Lord of the universe, we receive infinite, eternal value and strength. No wonder worship fills our hearts with joy!

Lord of the universe, I believe that in You I find my worth. Teach me to enter into a worship relationship with You, one that continues on in the background of my heart and mind, no matter what I'm doing throughout the day.

Believe in God's Wisdom and Power!

"To God belong wisdom and power; counsel and understanding are his."
JOB 12:13 NIV

Our belief in God is the foundation of our lives—and that foundation will grow stronger and steadier the more we get to know God. One way to do this is through regular Bible study, where we'll find that God is not only omnipotent (all-powerful) but also omniscient (all-knowing).

The word *wisdom* comes from the same ancient root words that had to do with vision, the ability to see into a deeper, spiritual reality. Where else can we turn for the insight to see beneath life's surface except to God? Who else can we believe is strong enough and wise enough to lead us through this life and into our eternal home?

God, I believe You are the source of all wisdom. I trust You to always guide me along paths of peace, joy, and love.

Vulnerability and Belief

*Behold, You desire truth in the inward parts, and in
the hidden part You will make me to know wisdom.*

PSALM 51:6 NKJV

Sometimes, we are like Adam and Eve in the garden after they had sinned: we are afraid to come naked and vulnerable into God's presence. We believe if we can hide ourselves from Him, we won't have to face our own faults and failure. But God cannot teach our hearts if we refuse to be open with Him. Our fear holds us back from the complete faith and belief that would allow us to give ourselves totally to God. We must take the risk of stepping into His presence with total honesty and utter vulnerability. When we do, His love touches us at our deepest, most secret places, the dark corners of our hearts we keep hidden even from those who know and love us best. God doesn't stop there, though. He goes even further and shares with us the riches of His wisdom.

*Beloved Lord, I believe I am safe with You, even if I expose to
You the parts of myself that make me most ashamed. I know
Your love is big enough to reach past all my defenses and
inadequacies. Thank You for sharing Yourself with me.*

Optimism and Belief

A cheerful look brings joy to the heart;
good news makes for good health.
PROVERBS 15:30 NLT

Medical experts indicate that it *does* matter whether you believe the proverbial glass is half-empty or half-full. Research has found that positive thinking leads to lower rates of depression, increased life span, and a reduced risk of death from heart disease. Consequently, many health professionals urge their patients to cultivate optimistic attitudes—and the Bible recommends this also.

This doesn't mean you'll automatically get everything you wish for; this recommendation isn't about finding a way to satisfy your every selfish whim. Instead, it has to do with your basic beliefs about reality: Do you believe life is filled with goodness—or do you see only the pain and suffering? To correct your beliefs so that they line up with the Bible's teachings, you may need to practice searching for the good news in your life every day. You might even make daily lists in a journal so that you more easily remember the many blessings God gives to you.

God, I believe You have given me so many reasons to be happy. Teach me to focus on these things, rather than on the things that irritate me or cause me pain. May my belief in Your love open my heart to Your blessing.

Carried in God's Arms

*"There you saw how the L*ORD *your God carried you, as a father carries his son, all the way you went until you reached this place."*
DEUTERONOMY 1:31 NIV

The old poem "Footprints in the Sand" describes a metaphorical situation where someone sees only one set of footsteps along the beach and believes God has abandoned them—when in reality, the single set of prints indicates the stretches in the journey when God was carrying them in His arms. In this passage from Deuteronomy, the Israelites found themselves in a similar state of disbelief. They were right up to the border of the Promised Land, with their toes practically hanging over the edge, but they were getting cold feet about going any farther. They doubted that God would be with them if they ventured into this new territory. But Moses reminded them that for forty long years God had carried them across the desert from Egypt.

A God who is strong enough to carry us through all we faced in the past is strong enough to keep His promises in the future. As we face new opportunities and dangers, He will never forsake us.

Faithful Lord, I believe You have carried me through the painful periods of my past, and I am confident You will never abandon me, either now or in the future.

False Beliefs

*"Look at you! You are putting your confidence
in a false belief that will not deliver you."*
JEREMIAH 7:8 NET

Our world is full of false beliefs—and all too easily they creep into our own hearts and minds. These beliefs can seem harmless, especially since so many people have them. The list of these deceptive beliefs is endless; here are just a few:

> *Money can buy happiness.*
> *I am unworthy of love.*
> *I have to be perfect in order to be worthy of others' respect.*
> *Material possessions can provide me with security.*
> *Some people are not worthy of my time or effort.*

Each one of these false beliefs is in direct opposition to what the Bible teaches about God and the life He wants us to live.

God, I believe Your Word is full of practical truth, truth I can live by—truth that will lead me not only to eternal life but to a healthier, fuller life now. May I not ignore the false beliefs that sneak into my head. Root them out, I pray. Make me sensitive to their presence, for I know they have the power to negatively shape my life and cloud my relationship with You.

The Work of Belief

When you received God's message. . .you accepted it not as a human message, but as it truly is, God's message, which is at work among you who believe.

1 THESSALONIANS 2:13 NET

The Bible is full of messages from God—promises of His love, His blessing, His protection, and His guidance. These messages have the power to work in your heart and in your life, changing you from the inside out. According to *HELPS Word-Studies*, the word *believe* as it's used in this verse has to do with "the believing that leads to and proceeds from God's inbirthing of faith." This is the ongoing, cyclical work of belief: your initial belief opened you up to God's messages; those messages then strengthened and deepened your belief; then, as your faith in God grew, you experienced more and more of His blessings; those blessings further expanded your faith, allowing you to experience even *more* divine blessing. . .and on and on the cycle goes, working over and over within you. God's messages will *never* stop their creative work of love!

I believe in You, Lord. You have blessed me again and again. Continue Your work in me, I pray. I want to continue to grow in faith. I want to become all You created me to be.

Scripture Index

More Inspiration for Your Beautiful Soul

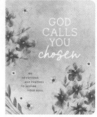

God Calls You Worthy
978-1-64352-474-0

God Calls You Loved
978-1-64352-804-5

God Calls You Forgiven
978-1-64352-637-9

God Calls You Chosen
978-1-64352-926-4

God Calls You Beautiful
978-1-64352-710-9

These delightful devotionals—created just for you—will encourage and inspire your soul with deeply rooted truths from God's Word.

Flexible Casebound / $12.99 each